Corrective Reading

M000011538

Word-Attack Basics

Siegfried Engelmann • Linda Carnine • Gary Johnson

SRA McGraw-Hill

Columbus, Ohio

A Division of The McGraw·Hill Companies

SRA/McGraw-Hill

A Division of The McGraw·Hill Companies

Printed in the United States of America.

Send all inquiries to:
SRA/McGraw-Hill
8787 Orion Place
Columbus, Ohio 43240-4027

ISBN 0-02-674772-3

3 4 5 6 7 8 9 10 DBH 04 03 02 01 00

Acknowledgments

The authors wish to thank the teachers, teacher-trainers, members of the Association for Direct Instruction, and SRA consultants who provided feedback on the 1988 edition and suggestions for the 1999 edition. We thank Barbara Johnson and her colleagues at the Monterey (CA) Special Education Local Plan Area (SELPA) office who provided sample Individual Reading Progress Charts that we adapted for this edition.

Contents

Contents

SRA's Corrective Reading Series:

SRA's *Corrective Reading* programs are divided into two strands: Decoding and Comprehension.

A single-strand sequence places students in one strand (**Decoding,** for example), and the students move through the strand from the point of initial placement (**Decoding A, B1, B2, or C**) to the end of the strand (**Decoding C**).

The double-strand sequence requires that students receive two full periods of instruction each day—one period in a Decoding program and one period in a Comprehension program.

Each Decoding program is designed to be used independently. Students may be placed at the beginning of one program and complete all the lessons in that program in either a single-strand or double-strand sequence.

Decoding Strand: A, B1, B2, C

Here is a diagram of the four decoding programs in SRA's *Corrective Reading* series.

Decoding A	Decoding B1	Decoding B2	Decoding C
65 lessons	65 lessons	65 lessons	125 lessons

Decoding A is appropriate for students in the second half of grade 3 through high school who virtually lack decoding skills. These students may recognize a few words, but functionally they are nonreaders.

Decoding B1 is appropriate for most problem readers in grades 3 through 12. They guess at words. They have trouble reading words such as **what, that, a,** and **the** when the words appear in a sentence context. They often read synonyms or printed words and are generally inconsistent in their reading behavior (reading a word correctly one time and missing it the next time).

Decoding B2 is appropriate for students in grades 4 through 12 who have some decoding problems, who do not read at an adequate rate, who still tend to confuse words with similar spellings, and who tend to make word-guessing mistakes.

Decoding C is appropriate for students who have mastered many basic reading skills but who have trouble with multisyllabic words and typical textbook material.

A reproducible copy of the **Corrective Reading** Decoding Placement Test and details on how to administer it appear in Appendix A at the end of this guide. The individually administered test measures each student's reading accuracy and oral-reading rate. Placement takes into account a student's ability to decode words in sentences and stories.

Progress Through the Decoding Strand

The Decoding programs are designed so that there is a careful progression of skill development from level to level. The Decoding strand has four entry points.

1 Students who begin at Level A should complete A and B1 in a school year (a total of 130 lessons).

2 Students who begin at Level B1 should complete B1 and B2 in a school year (a total of 130 lessons).

3 Students who begin at Level B2 should complete B2 and most of Level C in a school year.

4 Students who begin at Level C should complete C and additional outside reading in a school year.

Features of All Decoding Levels

Each level of SRA's **Corrective Reading** decoding programs has features that have been demonstrated through research studies to be effective in improving student performance.

◆ Each level is a core program, not ancillary material. Each level contains all the material you need and provides students with all the practice they need to learn the skills.

◆ All words, skills, and decoding strategies are taught through DIRECT INSTRUCTION. This approach is the most efficient for communicating with the students, for evaluating their performance on a moment-to-moment basis, and for achieving student mastery. Students are not simply exposed to skills. Skills are taught.

◆ Students are taught everything that is required for what they are to do later. Conversely, they are not taught skills that are not needed for later skill applications. The levels concentrate only on the necessary skills, not the nuances.

◆ Each level is based on cumulative skill development. Skills and strategies are taught, with lots of examples. Once a skill or strategy is taught, students receive practice in applying that skill until the end of the level. This type of cumulative development has been demonstrated by research studies to be the most effective method for teaching skills so that they become well learned or automatic.

◆ Because of the cumulative development of skills, the difficulty of material increases gradually but steadily.

◆ Each level is divided into daily lessons that can usually be presented in a class period (35–45 minutes of teacher-directed work and independent student applications).

- Each level contains Mastery Tests or Individual Reading Checkouts. These tests and checkouts are criterion-referenced performance measures of student **reading behavior.** These measures are part of the lessons. They provide you with very detailed data on student reading performance. They also show the students how their performance is improving as they progress through the program.

- Each level includes an effective management system. Students earn points for performance on each part of the daily lesson. Records of this performance may be used for awarding grades and documenting progress in specific skill areas.

- Each lesson specifies both teacher and student behavior. The lessons are scripted. The scripts specify what you do and say as well as appropriate student responses. The scripted lessons assure that you will (a) use uniform wording, (b) present examples in a manner that communicates effectively with students, and (c) be able to complete a lesson during a class period.

Facts About the Problem Reader

The series is designed to change the behavior of the problem reader. The specific decoding tendencies of the problem reader suggest what a program must do to be effective in changing this student's behavior.

The problem reader makes frequent word-identification errors. The student makes a higher percentage of mistakes when reading connected sentences than when reading words in word lists. Often, the student can read words correctly in word lists but then misidentifies the same words when they are embedded in connected sentences.

The specific mistakes the reader makes include word omissions, word additions, and confusion of high-frequency words, such as **what** and **that, of** and **for, and** and **the.** The student also reads synonyms (saying "pretty" for **beautiful**). The student often guesses at words, basing the guess on the word's beginning or ending. And the student is consistently inconsistent, making a mistake on one word in a sentence and then making a different mistake when re-reading the sentence.

The student doesn't seem to understand the relationship between the arrangement of letters in a word and the pronunciation of the word. Often, the student is confused about the "word meaning" (a fact suggested by "synonym reading," "opposite reading," and word guessing). The strategy seems to be based on rules the student has been taught. The problem reader follows such advice as: "Look at the beginning of the word and take a guess," "Think of what the word might mean," and "Look at the general shape of the word." The result is a complicated strategy that is often backwards: The student seems to think that to read a word, one must first "understand" the word, then select the spoken word that corresponds to that understanding.

Although the problem reader may use a strategy that is "meaning based," the reader is often preempted from comprehending passages. The reason is that the student doesn't read a passage with the degree of accuracy needed to understand what the passage actually says. (Omitting the word **not** from one sentence changes the meaning dramatically.)

Furthermore, the student's reading rate is often inadequate, making it difficult for the student to remember the various details of the passage, even if they were decoded accurately. Often, the problem reader doesn't have an effective reading comprehension strategy because the student's poor decoding and slow rate don't make the material sensible.

Finally, the poor reader is not a highly motivated student. For this student, reading has been punishing. The student often professes indifference: "I don't care if I can read or not." But the student's behavior gives strong suggestions that the student cares a great deal.

The student's ineffective reading strategies and negative attitudes about reading become more ingrained as the reader gets older. To overcome them requires a very careful program, one that systematically replaces the strategies with new ones and that provides lots and lots of practice.

The procedures that are used in the program derive directly from the difficulties that students have with particular tasks. Based on the problems students have, we can identify two major levels of difficulty. The less difficult level is reading isolated words. The more difficult level is reading words that are in a connected sentence context.

Isolated words are easier because they do not prompt the student to use inappropriate guessing strategies that the student applies when reading connected sentences. When the student reads word lists, therefore, the student is not as likely to guess on the basis of the order of the preceding words, or on the basis of images that are prompted by preceding words. Not all word lists are the same level of difficulty.

Less difficult lists require reading words that have similar parts. More difficult lists require reading words that do not have similar parts. This type of list is sometimes called a "mixed list" because all types of words appear in it.

Reading words in connected sentences is more difficult than reading words in isolation. The task of reading a particular passage can be made relatively more difficult or less difficult.

Passage reading is less difficult if the student has read the passage and received feedback on all errors.

Passage reading is more difficult if the student is reading the passage for the first time.

Lessons in the Decoding programs are designed to give students practice that leads them to become stronger in what is easier for them to do and that gives them progressive practice in the more difficult reading endeavors. The lessons do this while remaining within the skill limits of the student, which means that an appropriately placed student will not be overwhelmed with difficult tasks or bored by tasks that are too easy.

Each lesson presents words in isolation and gives students practice with easier lists and more difficult lists. When new words are introduced, they often appear in lists of words that have similar parts. In later lessons, these same words appear in mixed lists where the students must rely more on the decoding skills taught earlier. Except for the early lessons in Level A, all Decoding lessons provide students practice with reading familiar words in sentence contexts.

The procedures require the students to read sentences or passages and then re-read them. In Level C, students keep a record of their performance on the individual timed reading, called an Individual Reading Checkout. Their improved performance on the timed reading provides students with evidence of their ability to retain and apply the decoding skills they have been taught.

The structure of the lessons addresses the student's skill deficiencies directly but positively, in a manner that provides the type of practice students need to relearn fundamental strategies and to learn new skills, and that does not overwhelm them with material or rules that result in a high rate of errors.

The Problems

An effective corrective reading program must address the specific needs of the problem reader.

1 The learner must learn to look at the order of letters in a word and learn that this order suggests the general pronunciation of the word. Furthermore, the student must learn that the game is simple: first figure out how the letters suggest to *say* the word. Then see if the word you say is one that you recognize, one that has meaning. (Note that this strategy is basically the opposite of the one the typical problem reader uses.)

2 The problem reader must receive practice in reading connected sentences that are composed of words that have been taught in isolation. Merely because the student reads words in lists does not imply transfer to written sentences.

3 The student must receive strong reinforcement for working on reading because the task is very difficult and frustrating for the student. The student has received a great deal of evidence that reading is a puzzle that can't seem to be solved.

4 Finally, the student must receive practice in reading a variety of passages. If the student practices reading only narrative passages, the student will not "automatically" transfer the reading skills to textbooks, articles, or other forms of expository writing. Therefore, different styles must be introduced.

The Solutions

SRA's **Corrective Reading** decoding programs are successful with problem readers because they provide the careful integration, the practice, and the management details that the problem reader needs to succeed.

The student receives daily practice in oral reading, with immediate feedback. (Only through oral reading can we discover what the student is actually reading.)

The student reads word lists with information about how to pronounce various letter combinations, such as **th** and **or**. The student also reads sentences and passages composed of words that have been taught. The sentences and passages are designed so that they are relatively easy if the student approaches words as entities that are to be analyzed according to the arrangement of letters, but difficult if the student guesses on the basis of the context or syntax of the sentence. (The sentences are designed so that guesses often lead to an incorrect identification of the word.)

The Mastery Tests and checkouts in the series assure that the student observes progress in reading rate and reading

accuracy. The series presents comprehension items in a way that demonstrates the relationship between what is decoded and how it is to be understood. Initially, the comprehension activities are deliberately separated from the decoding activities so that the student's misconceptions about reading are not exaggerated. The comprehension activities, however, show the student that what is read is to be understood.

Finally, the series addresses the problem reader's poor self-image. The series is designed so the student can succeed in real reading tasks. Furthermore, a point system that is based on realistic performance goals assures that the reader who tries will succeed and will receive reinforcement for improved performance.

In summary, the series uses a two-pronged approach. Each level teaches effective reading skills to replace the student's ineffective approach to reading. Each level also contains an effective management system that turns students on to reading. This turn-on is not achieved by "seducing" the reader with entertaining topics, but by rewarding the reader for steady improvement in reading performance. The approach WORKS.

Introduction to the 1999 Edition

The 1999 edition of **Decoding A** has a number of changes designed to make the teacher material easier to use and the student materials more attractive for students.

The Program—Decoding A Word-Attack Basics

The first level of the decoding programs in **SRA's *Corrective Reading*** series is **Decoding A** *Word-Attack Basics.*

Who It's For

Decoding A is designed for very poor readers in grades 3 through 12. The program is appropriate for students who understand English and whose scores on the ***Corrective Reading*** placement test indicate that they belong in the program.

The program is not meant to be used with students who do not speak any English, or whose grasp of English is quite weak.

Decoding A works effectively with students who would traditionally be identified as learning disabled, educationally handicapped, or perceptually handicapped. The program can also be used with adults who have received some reading instruction but who have never learned to decode accurately. As long as students demonstrate the skill level necessary to enter the program, they may be placed in the program.

What Is Taught

The following skills are taught in **Decoding A.**

◆ Identifying the sounds of letters

◆ Sounding out words that are presented orally and then saying them fast

◆ Sounding out and identifying written words that are spelled regularly

◆ Decoding irregularly spelled words

◆ Reading words "the fast way"

◆ Reading sentences

◆ Reading short selections

◆ Spelling

Related skills such as matching, word completion (for example, rhyming), and symbol scanning are included in the student Workbook pages.

Upon completion of the program, students should be able to do the following activities.

◆ Read sentences such as "She was a master at planting trees." These sentences are composed primarily of regularly spelled words (containing as many as six sounds).

◆ Read short selections, such as the following:

> **Ten men got in a truck.**
> **They went to the creek and set up a tent.**
> **How can ten men fit in the tent?**
> **They can not.**
> **Six men will sleep under a tree.**

◆ Read common irregular words, such as **what, was, do, said, to, of, said,** and **you,** with only infrequent errors.

◆ Read words that begin with difficult letter combinations, such as **st, bl, sl, fl, pl, sw, cl, tr,** and **dr.**

◆ Read words that end with difficult letter combinations, such as **nt, nd, st, ts, mp, ps, cks, ls, ms, th, er, ing, ers,** and **y.**

◆ Pronounce commonly confused word parts, such as the **k** sound in **trick,** the **e** sound in **set,** and the **s** ending sound in **mats, runs,** and **munches.**

◆ Spell simple words that have a clear sound-symbol relationship (including words that contain **th, wh, sh, ch,** and various other letter combinations).

◆ Independently perform various simple activities such as matching sounds and completing words with missing letters.

Decoding A provides the foundation skills that are built upon in the later decoding programs, **Decoding B1, Decoding B2,** and **Decoding C.** These programs broaden the base of students' decoding skills and provide the type of practice that students need to read a variety of text and narrative materials both accurately and rapidly.

Note: A more detailed list of behavioral objectives appears in Appendix C of this guide.

The Materials

The program consists of this Teacher's Guide, two Teacher Presentation Books, Examiner's Manual with Test Booklets for mid-program and end-of-program evaluation, and a Workbook for each student.

This guide contains basic information about the program and specific information for presenting exercises and for correcting mistakes.

Teacher Presentation Book A1 covers Lessons 1–30; Book A2 covers Lessons 31–65. The Teacher Presentation Books contain a script for each lesson and answer keys for the student Workbook. Scripts specify what you say and do and what the students say.

◆ This blue type indicates what you say.

◆ (This type indicates what you do.)

◆ *This italic type shows the students' response.*

The following sample from Lesson 29 demonstrates how the type is used. Note that correction procedures are indicated by a double vertical bar at the left.

━━━━━━ **EXERCISE 5** ━━━━━━

SPELLING FROM DICTATION
1. Touch part 1 in your Workbook. ✔ You're going to write words that I dictate.
2. First word: **this.** What word? (Signal.) *This.* Listen again: **thththĭĭĭsss.** Write it in the first blank. (Check work and correct.)
   To correct:
   a. Say the sounds in **this.** Get ready.
   b. Show me the letters for **ththth.** (Check work and correct.) Show me the letter for **ĭĭĭ.** (Check work and correct.) Show me the letter for **sss.** (Check work and correct.)
3. Next word: **the.** What word? (Signal.) *The.* Listen again: **ththth . . . ēēē.** Write it in the next blank. (Check work and correct.)
4. (Repeat step 3 for **that, he, she, dad.**)

The Workbook contains pages for 65 lessons. A daily Point Chart provides a record of the student's performance for each lesson. A Point Summary Chart and a Progress Graph are on the inside front and back covers of the Workbook.

Scheduling and Grouping

Here are general considerations for scheduling and grouping students in the program.

1 A lesson should be presented every day at an assigned time.

2 The lesson will take between 30 and 45 minutes, depending on the size of the group.

3 The students are best served if there are no more than 12 in a group.

4 The program can be used with individual students in resource-room settings, in which case it will take less time to present each lesson.

Placement

A reproducible copy of the *Corrective Reading* decoding placement test and details on how to administer it appear in Appendix A at the end of this guide. The individually administered test measures each student's reading accuracy and oral reading rate. Placement takes into account a student's ability to decode words in isolation and words in stories.

Retesting

Some students will perform much better in the program than their placement test performance indicates. Typically, these students do very poorly on the test, but during the daily lessons, they perform quite well, reading rather fluently, making practically no errors, and generally behaving as if they have been placed in the wrong program.

Watch for such students and retest them as soon as it becomes apparent that their test performance did not accurately indicate their ability. Frequently, their performance on the retest will place them in **Decoding B1.**

Mastery Tests

There are 12 in-program Mastery Tests in the Decoding A progam. These tests provide information about student performance and indicate remedies for groups or students who have not mastered specific reading skills. For further details, see the section of the guide entitled "In–Program Mastery Tests."

There are also a separate Examiner's Manual and Mastery Tests that you may use after Lesson 20, Lesson 45, and Lesson 65. See the Decoding A Examiner's Manual for further details.

The Lesson

Each of the 65 lessons in **Decoding A** is divided into three major parts.

❶ Word-Attack Skills

❷ Workbook Exercises

❸ Individual Reading Checkouts

The daily lesson is designed for a period of 30 to 45 minutes.

Word-Attack Skills take up the first 15 minutes of the period. They are orally presented exercises or written exercises that teach specific skills. New skills are usually introduced at the beginning of a lesson.

Workbook Exercises reinforce the skills presented in the Word-Attack Exercises. Some activities, such as word reading, sentence reading, and story reading, are directed by the teacher. Other activities are done independently by students. The Workbook Exercises require 10 to 15 minutes.

The last segment of the lesson is the **Individual Reading Checkout,** which requires from 1 to 5 minutes for each student. During this part of the lesson, the student reads a group of words, sentences, or a story read earlier by the group. The Individual Reading Checkouts provide reading practice and reinforce skills students have been taught.

Management of the program is aided by using a point system. Students receive points for successful performance in (a) the Word-Attack Skills, (b) the independent Workbook Exercises, and (c) the Individual Reading Checkout.

The points earned are recorded at the top of each daily Workbook lesson. The charts on the inside front and back covers of the

Workbook provide a permanent, ongoing record of the student's performance.

Typical students placed in **Decoding A** are turned off to formal instruction. Therefore, the management system of the program is very important, because it shows students that though they will have to work hard, when they do, they will achieve. The management system provides both a graphic demonstration that learning is taking place and a basis for grading students fairly.

Summary of Lesson Parts

Follow this sequence for each lesson.

❶ Present the Word-Attack Exercises. These are the first four to six exercises in the lesson.

❷ Award points to students for performance on the Word-Attack Exercises. A note appears in every lesson indicating the end of the word-attack section and reminding you to award points.

❸ Present the Workbook Exercises. Starting with Lesson 18, you direct the sentence/story reading with the group.

❹ Check those sections of the Workbook pages that had been assigned as independent work, and award points for performance on those activities. The Workbook checkouts begin in Lesson 4.

❺ Conduct the Individual Reading Checkouts. Each student will read a group of words in Lessons 1 through 22, a series of sentences in Lessons 23 through 29, and a short selection in Lessons 30 through 65. (Beginning with Lesson 46, the reading is timed.)

6 Students' point totals for the lesson are computed and entered in a box at the top of the Workbook lesson. Students also record their total points on their Point Summary Charts.

Familiarize yourself with this sequence. Examine Lesson 1 both in the Teacher Presentation Book and in the Workbook. Note where each step takes place.

General Information

Introducing the Program

During the first class meeting, make these points to the students.

1 They will be involved in a program that will teach them beginning decoding skills. They will be able to succeed in this program.

2 There is a two-way agreement: You will work very hard to do the best job you can of teaching. However, they must follow the rules and work hard also.

3 They will be able to earn points for each of the three parts of the lesson.

  a. They can earn as many as 4 points for the word-attack portion of the lesson.

  b. They can earn as many as 5 points for doing their Workbook pages well.

  c. They can earn as many as 4 points for Individual Reading Checkouts.

You may also tell them that their grades are based on their performance, and that if they work hard, they will be able to earn A's.

Setup for the Lesson

Make sure students are seated so that all of them are able to see every sound and word you point to in your presentation book. Lower-performing students and students whose behavior poses problems should be seated directly in front of you so that you can monitor their responses. Assign permanent seats if possible.

Have student Workbooks and pencils arranged so that you can pass them out immediately after the word-attack exercises.

Pacing the Exercises

Because you must teach a great deal of information during the daily presentation, it is important that you move quickly, but not so quickly that students make mistakes.

To ensure a smoothly paced lesson, become familiar with the exercises you are presenting. You must be able to present them without referring to the page for every word you say.

Talk as if you're conveying something important. Say your lines quickly. Don't drag out the instructions. If you are slow, students' attention will wander.

Signals

When you present Word-Attack Exercises, all students should respond *on signal.* This means that the group responds in unison when you signal. By listening carefully to the responses, you can tell which students make mistakes and which ones respond late, copying those who responded first. As a result, you'll be able to correct specific mistakes, maximize the amount of practice, and evaluate the performance of each student.

Here are the rules for effective signaling.

1 Never signal while you are talking. Talk first, and then signal.

2 The time interval between the last word of your instructions and the signal should always be about 1 second. Signals should be timed so that students can respond together.

The hand-drop signal is used for tasks that you present orally. Follow these steps to execute this signal.

1 Hold your hand out (as if you're stopping traffic) while you are saying the instructions or presenting the question.

2 Continue to hold your hand still for 1 second after you have completed the instructions or the question.

3 Then quickly drop your hand. Students should respond the instant your hand drops.

The point-touch signal is used when you point to words or symbols in the presentation book or on the chalkboard. Here are the steps:

1 Hold your finger about an inch from the page or chalkboard, just below the symbol. (Be careful not to cover or obscure the symbol from any student's view.)

2 As you point, present the instructions or question (for example, What sound?)

3 Continue pointing for 1 second after completing the question or instruction.

4 Quickly touch just under the symbol. (Don't touch the symbol itself, and don't touch so far below it that there may be a question about which symbol is to be identified.) Students should respond the instant your finger touches the page.

Using these signals may seem awkward at first, but with practice you'll be able to execute clear signals and receive useful feedback from the students. The hand-drop and point-touch are the most common signals in **Decoding A.** Other signals are explained in specific discussions later in this guide.

Corrections

All students will make mistakes. These mistakes provide you with valuable information about the difficulties the students are having. Knowing how to correct effectively is essential to successful teaching.

Mistakes should be corrected immediately. For some activities, specific corrections are specified in the Teacher Presentation Book. All follow the same general format:

1 You say the correct answer as soon as you hear a mistake.

2 You repeat the task that was missed. For instance, if students responded incorrectly when you pointed to **s** and asked What sound? you tell them the answer (step 1). The sound is **sss.** Then you repeat the task (step 2). What sound?

3 You return to the first task in the sequence. (If students miss the sound **s,** you return to the first sound in the group of sounds.)

4 You repeat the exercises until the students can perform on all tasks without a mistake.

Here's the entire correction:

Teacher	Students
(Points to **s**.) What sound? (Signal.)	No response.
1. The sound is **sss**.	
2. What sound? (Signal.)	*sss*.
3. Good. Remember, this is **sss**. Back to the beginning.	
4. (Points to **m**.) What sound? (Signal.)	*mmm*.
(Points to **r**.) What sound? (Signal.)	*rrr*.
(Points to **s**.) What sound? (Signal.)	*sss*.
Good remembering **sss**.	
(Points to **a**.) What sound? (Signal.)	*ăăă*.

Teaching to Criterion

At the conclusion of any task, each student should be able to respond immediately without making any mistakes. Your goal as a teacher should be to see that students are "firm"—that is, meet this criterion.

Let students know what you expect of them. Keep on a task until you can honestly say to them Great. Everybody read every word correctly. If your criterion for a task is strict, the group will have less difficulty with similar tasks in subsequent lessons.

Formats

In the following discussion of the lesson presentation, the term *format* will be used. A format is an exercise set up in a specific form. Here is a format for word reading.

WORD READING

Task A Meet

1. You're going to read each word. First you sound it out; then you say it fast.
2. (Touch the ball of the arrow for the first word.) Sound it out. Get ready. (Touch under **m, ee, t**.) *mmmēēēt*. (Repeat until the students say the sounds without pausing.)
3. Again. Sound it out. Get ready. (Touch under **m, ee, t**.) *mmmēēēt*. (Repeat until firm.)
4. (Touch the ball of the arrow.) Say it fast. (Slash right, along the arrow.) *Meet*. Yes, **meet**.

Simply by replacing the word **meet,** we can create many other exercises that follow the same format and that would be presented in the same way. All exercises in **Decoding A** are in formats. The following are the advantages of format exercises.

1 They are easy to present because your behavior in the basic steps remains the same for all examples of a given format.

2 They are easy for students to comprehend because the directions and wording are the same for all examples of a particular format.

Some formats are presented for 20 or more lessons; other formats, in only two or three lessons. **A large blue dot next to a heading in the lesson presentation indicates the introduction of a new format. This signals that there is a significant change in the method in which you are to present a task.**

Word-Attack Skills

Only the major formats are discussed in this guide. They are grouped according to the skills they teach; for example, the major sound-identification formats are presented first, followed by pronunciation formats. You should practice the formats before beginning the program or before teaching a lesson in which a new skill is introduced.

Sound Identification

Lessons 1–65

There is a sound-identification exercise in every lesson. The following chart shows how each sound is pronounced and the lesson in which each sound is introduced.

Sound	As In	Type	Lesson
m	mat	continuous	1
a	and	continuous	1
s	sat	continuous	1
ē	eat	continuous	1
t	tap	stop	1
r	run	continuous	2
d	dad	stop	3
i	if	continuous	4
f	fin	continuous	6
h	hat	stop	7
c	cat	stop	8
th	this	continuous	9
sh	she	continuous	12
n	not	continuous	14
o	ox	continuous	18
ing	sing	continuous	22

Sound	As In	Type	Lesson
g	go	stop	22
e	end	continuous	23
k	kick	stop	27
ck	kick	stop	27
w	we	continuous	31
wh	why	continuous	31
ō	over	continuous	32
l	lip	continuous	33
ol	old	continuous	35
or	for	continuous	35
er	her	continuous	36
p	pat	stop	38
u	up	continuous	39
x	ox	continuous	41
b	bag	stop	44
y	yes	continuous	46
ch	chomp	stop	51
j	jump	stop	54
v	very	continuous	56
z	zoo	continuous	59
qu	quick	continuous	62

The purpose of the sound-identification exercises is to teach a specific sound for each symbol. Students will use the sounds when they sound out and spell words. Only the most commonly used sound is introduced for each symbol, except that two sounds are introduced for **o** and **e.**

There are four basic sound-identification formats. Some introduce new sounds; others review and firm sounds that have been taught previously.

LESSON 1 Sound Introduction

The first sound-identification format introduces the sounds **s, a, t, e,** and **m.**

━━━━━━━ EXERCISE 2 ━━━━━━━

● **SOUND INTRODUCTION**

1. My turn. I'll touch these letters and say the sounds.
2. (Point to **s.** Pause. Touch under **s.** Say:) sss. (Point to **a.** Pause. Touch under **a.** Say:) ăăă. (Point to **t.** Pause. Touch under **t.** Say:) t. (Point to **e.** Pause. Touch under **e.** Say:) ēēē. (Point to **m.** Pause. Touch under **m.** Say:) mmm.
3. Your turn. Say each sound when I touch it.
4. (Point to **s.**) What sound? (Touch under **s.**) The students say: *sss.*
5. (Repeat step 4 for each remaining letter.)

To correct:
   a. (Say the sound loudly as soon as you hear an error.)
   b. (Point to the sound.) This sound is ——. What sound? (Touch under the letter.)
   c. (Repeat the series of letters until all the students can correctly identify all the sounds in order.)

s a t
e m

Teaching Techniques. In step 2 you model the sounds. In steps 3 through 5 you test students on the sounds.

Remember to follow the point-touch signaling techniques in steps 2, 4, and 5. When you point to a letter, make sure students are looking at that letter. Say What sound? Pause for 1 second before you touch just under the letter. For continuous sounds such as **m, a, s,** and **e,** hold the sound for about 2 seconds. For stop sounds such as **t, d,** and **p,** touch the letter for only an instant, and make sure students say "t," not "tuh." Practice the sounds before presenting the lesson.

Corrections. Treat both early and late responses as errors. If students respond before you signal, say You're early. Repeat the pointing and touching until they respond on signal.

Also treat late responses as errors. Say You've got to say the sound as soon as I touch it. Repeat the signal until all students are responding on signal.

If students misidentify a sound, follow the correction procedure specified in the exercise. Then repeat the entire series of letters until all students correctly identify all the sounds in sequence. This step is very important. If you simply correct the mistake and then continue to the next sound, you don't know if students can actually discriminate the missed sound from other sounds. You know they are firm only if they can respond correctly to all the sounds. For some groups, this may mean repeating the sequence of sounds five times or more. Provide the needed repetition. Tell the students That was pretty good. Let's try it again. This time I want to hear everybody say every sound correctly.

Note that the correction procedure in the exercise appears in only the first 11 lessons; however, you will use the correction for sound-identification errors throughout the program.

Remember that the goal of corrections is not to punish students but to firm the responses of those who need practice.

Individual Test. The basic test of students' performance is the individual test that appears at the end of the exercise. Do not omit this activity. If some consistently miss sounds while others are firm, ask only the poor performers to repeat the series. For example, say This time, Harold, James, and Denise, say all the sounds.

LESSON 25 Sound Identification ē, ĕ

Two sounds for the letter **e** are contrasted in this format. The first sound taught for the letter is **ēēē** (as in **see**). This sound was introduced first because (a) it is easier to pronounce, (b) it occurs in many common simple words, such as **he, she,** and **me,** and (c) it is less similar to the sound **ĭĭĭ** (as in **if**), which is introduced in Lesson 4.

Lesson 23 teaches the other sound for **e** (as in **end**). Lesson 25 is the first sound-identification exercise in which the two pronunciations for the letter **e** are used.

================ EXERCISE 1 ================

● **SOUND IDENTIFICATION**
1. (Point to **e.**) Listen. You learned two sounds for this letter. One sound is the letter name. That's **ēēē.** You say **ēēē** when you say the alphabet. The other sound is **ĕĕĕ.** That's not the letter name. Your turn.
2. One sound is the letter name. What's that sound? (Touch.) *ēēē.* Yes, **ēēē.** And what's the other sound? (Touch.) *ĕĕĕ.* Yes, **ĕĕĕ.**
3. (Repeat step 2 until firm.)
4. Say each sound when I touch it.
5. (Point to **th.**) What sound? (Touch.) *thththt.* Yes, **thththt.**
6. (Repeat step 5 for **s, ă, c, sh, t, ĭ, g, ŏ, r, f.**)

Individual test

I'll call on different students to say all the sounds. If everybody I call on can say all the sounds without making a mistake, we'll go on to the next exercise. (Call on two or three students. Touch under each sound. Each student says all the sounds.)

e th

s a c

sh t i

g o r f

Corrections. Some students may have trouble saying the sound **ĕĕĕ** (as in **end**). Also, the fact that there are two sounds for **e** may confuse them.

Correct problems in identifying the sound **ĕĕĕ** by saying Think of the word **end.** That word begins with the sound you want—**ĕĕĕ.** What sound?

Correct problems of confusing the two sounds by saying When you say the alphabet, what name do you call this letter? . . . What's the sound that's the same as the letter name?

If students continue to have trouble with this exercise, tell them you'll return to it later. After completing one or two other reading exercises, return to it.

LESSON 35 Sound Combination: ol

The sound combinations **th, sh,** and **wh** are introduced as "sounds." Starting with Lesson 35, the general procedure for introducing a sound combination is for the teacher to model the combination, such as **ol,** in isolation, then present a series of words that contain that combination. This procedure occurs in several consecutive lessons, followed by other lessons in which the newly taught combination appears in sound-identification exercises and in words.

Following is the sound-identification exercise from Lesson 35.

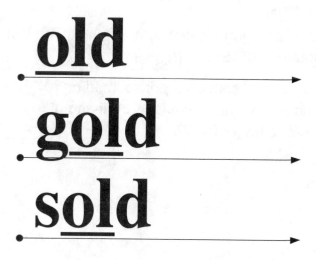

═══ **EXERCISE 3** ═══

ol

- **SOUND COMBINATION: ol**
1. (Point to **ol.**) These letters go together and say **ōōōlll.** What sound? (Signal.) **ōōōlll.**
2. You're going to read words that have the sound **ōōōlll.**
3. (Point to the underlined part of **old.**) What sound? (Touch.) **ōōōlll.** What word? (Signal.) *Old.*
4. (Repeat step 3 for **g<u>ol</u>d, s<u>ol</u>d.**)

<u>ol</u>d
g<u>ol</u>d
s<u>ol</u>d

Corrections. When you hear an error, immediately say the correct sound, sound combination, or word. Repeat the task the students missed. Then return to step 2 of the exercise and repeat the steps in sequence until students can perform without error on the entire exercise.

Pronunciations

Lessons 1–65

One of the major problems very poor decoders have is pronouncing words. Their pronunciation problems are numerous. For example, they may mispronounce vowels that occur in the middle of short words—particularly if the sound is ĭĭĭ (fill) or ĕĕĕ (set). They may have trouble with words that have s near or at the end—for example, fits, fist, and fins. Frequently, they'll have trouble saying words such as trip and trick.

In Lessons 1 through 5, students are taught to identify the sounds that compose words. You say a word, such as if, then identify the sounds.

The first sound is iii. Say it. (Signal.) The last sound is fff. Say it. (Signal.)

To signal a sound response, hold up a finger. Hold up one finger for iii and a second finger for fff.

Also beginning with Lesson 1, the students repeat words the teacher says. The objective of this exercise is to give students ample practice in *saying* words with specific vowel sounds before they are required to *read* words with those sounds. Next, students identify the middle sound (the vowel sound) in words that you give them. For example, What's the middle sound in seed?

Later in the program, you give students words that differ only in the middle sound (bean, ben, ban), and they are required to identify which word has a specified middle sound. Which word has the middle sound ăăă?

The final pronunciation exercise, appearing in Lessons 50 through 65, requires students to identify which of similar-sounding words have a given meaning. For example, after you present the words sleek and sleet, say One of those words means something that is very smooth. Which word? . . . One of those words means frozen rain. Which word?

LESSON 4 Pronunciations, Middle Sound

================ EXERCISE 7 ================

- **PRONUNCIATIONS**

1. Listen. We planted a **seed.** (Pause.)
   Seed. Say it. (Signal.) *Seed.*
2. I'll say the first sound in the word **sssēēēd.**
   (Pause.) **sss.** What's the first sound?
   (Signal.) *sss.* Yes, **sss.**
3. Say the middle sound in the word **sssēēēd.**
   Get ready. (Signal.) *ēēē.* Yes, *ēēē.*

   To correct:
   a. (Hold up one finger.) **sss.**
   b. (Hold up two fingers.) *ēēē.*
   c. What's the middle sound in **sssēēēd?**
      (Signal.) *ēēē.* Yes, *ēēē.*
   d. (Repeat step 3 until firm.)
4. Listen: **sad.** Say it. (Signal.) *Sad.*
5. I'll say the first sound in the word **sssăăăd.**
   (Pause.) **sss.** What's the first sound?
   (Signal.) *sss.* Yes, **sss.**
6. Say the middle sound in the word **sssăăăd.**
   Get ready. (Signal.) *ăăă.* Yes, *ăăă.*
7. One of those words has the middle sound
   ēēē. I'll say both words again: **seed** (pause)
   sad. Which word has the middle sound *ēēē?*
   (Signal.) *Seed.* Yes, **seed.**

Teaching Techniques. The signal used for all responses in this exercise is the hand drop.

In steps 1 and 4, listen carefully to students' pronunciation of the words. Frequently, students omit the ending sound, **d.** They should not say "seeduh" or "sadah"; however, the **d** sound must be audible.

This exercise should be paced relatively fast. There should be no great breaks between steps 1, 2, and 3, or between steps 4, 5, and 6. Practice each of these units so that you can present them quickly without constantly referring to the script.

When you say the words slowly in steps 3 and 6, do not pause between the sounds in the words. Simply slow down the pronunciation.

Step 7 is particularly difficult. Students will have less trouble if you pause before and after each word. I'll say both words again (pause) **seed** (pause) **sad.** Pause. Now quickly say Which word has the middle sound *ēēē?*

Corrections. Practice the correction that appears in the exercise. In steps a and b, say the first two sounds of the word without pausing between them: **sssēēē.** Hold up one finger when you say **sss** and hold up a second finger as soon as you begin to say *ēēē.* While holding up two fingers, quickly ask What's the middle sound in **sssēēēd?** If students continue to make the mistake, tell them the sound.

Finally, repeat step 3 of the exercise. Do not omit this part of the correction—it requires students to identify the middle sound without prompting.

Practice the basic procedure with the words **sad** and **seed.** Use the correction procedure for all errors the students make when they are asked to identify the middle sound.

LESSON 30 Pronunciations, Three Words

This exercise will be difficult for some students who may have trouble saying the three words and identifying the word with the specified middle sound.

Task D   Bean, ben, ban

1. Listen: **bean, ben, ban.** Say those words. (Signal.) *Bean, ben, ban.* (Repeat until firm.)
2. One of those words has the middle sound ăăă. I'll say the words again: **bean, ben, ban.** Which word has the middle sound ăăă? (Signal.) *Ban.* Yes, **ban.**
3. Which word has the middle sound ēēē? (Signal.) *Bean.* Yes, **bean.** Which word has the middle sound ĕĕĕ? (Signal.) *Ben.* Yes, **ben.**
4. Listen: **bēēēan.** What's the middle sound in the word **bean?** (Signal.) ēēē. Yes, ēēē. Listen: **bĕĕĕn.** What's the middle sound in the word **ben?** (Signal.) ĕĕĕ. Yes, ĕĕĕ. Listen: **băăăn.** What's the middle sound in the word **ban?** (Signal.) ăăă. Yes, ăăă.
5. (Repeat step 4 until firm.) Good job.

Teaching Techniques. Make sure that students are firm on step 1 before moving on in the exercise. Listen to their pronunciations. They must say words properly—with the sounds ēēē, ĕĕĕ, and ăăă clearly distinguishable.

In steps 2 and 3, hold the sounds ăăă, ēēē, and ĕĕĕ for at least 2 seconds. This will give students thinking time, and it will be easier for them to find the correct word. Practice this step: Which word has the middle sound ăăă? Pause 1 second and drop your hand. If you hurry this part of the exercise, students will tend to make mistakes.

Corrections. If students identify the wrong word, tell them the middle sound in the word they identified. For example:

Which word has the middle sound ēēē?

Students answer: *Ban.* **Ban** has the middle sound ăăă. Listen: **băăăn.** What middle sound? . . . But which word has the middle sound ēēē?

If students make mistakes on step 4, repeat the words after correcting a mistake. Students are considered firm on the exercise when you present the words in step 4 in sequence and they make no mistakes. Practice this correction before presenting Lesson 30. Use this correction procedure when students make mistakes identifying words with a specified middle sound.

Students may have the most difficulty with word pairs that involve the middle sounds ĭĭĭ and ĕĕĕ **(mitt, met).** You can reduce some of the problems they have with these words by making sure they (a) pronounce each word correctly and (b) understand the usage of the word.

If they have trouble saying a word such as **met,** give them a sentence containing the word. Listen: He **met** her. **Met.** What word? . . . He had a catcher's **mitt. Mitt.** What word? . . .

Also make sure you are pronouncing the word pairs so the middle sounds are distinguishable. If you pronounce **met** and **mitt** so that they sound the same, obviously students are going to have trouble.

Individual Tests. Although individual tests are not specified for the pronunciation formats, call on different students, particularly those who are having trouble, and ask them to pronounce the words. Some students require a great deal of practice before they are able to say the words correctly; you can identify these students more quickly through individual tests than in group reponses.

Summary

One reason students have trouble with reading is that they don't discriminate between different vowel sounds. The pronunciation exercises not only teach students the different pronunciations, but also lead them to realize that how a word is pronounced frequently tells how the word is spelled.

Do not expect students to master pronunciations immediately. Most students will require a great deal of practice—many repetitions—before they can easily pronounce certain words and identify the vowel sound in these words.

Say the Sounds

Lessons 1–10

There is one basic say-the-sounds format. You slowly say a word without pausing between the sounds. Listen: **ăăămmm.** Students slowly say the word with you. Then you tell them Say it fast.

The say-the-sounds exercises involve specific behaviors that are used in the word-reading exercises. The basic difference between the exercises is that say-the-sounds formats do not involve written symbols. They are purely oral activities, giving students practice in the oral steps of the reading procedure. Students say the word one sound at a time without pausing between the sounds, and then say the word the fast way.

EXERCISE 4

● **SAY THE SOUNDS**

> Note: Do not write the words on the board. This is an oral exercise.

Task A Eat

1. I'm going to say a word slowly without stopping. Then you'll say the word with me. First I'll say ēēēt slowly. (Hold up a finger for each sound. Do not stop between the two sounds.) ēēēt.
2. Everybody, say that with me. Get ready. (Hold up a finger for each sound. Say *ēēēt* with the students.)
3. All by yourselves. Get ready. (Hold up a finger for each sound.) *eeet.* (Repeat until the students say the sounds without stopping.)
4. Say it fast. (Signal.) *Eat.*
5. What word? (Signal.) *Eat.* Yes, **eat.**

Teaching Techniques. The signal used in steps 2 and 3 is the same as in the pronunciation track. Pause for 1 second after saying Get ready. Then hold up one finger for the ē in ēēē and a second finger for the **t** in ēēēt. Hold the ēēē sound for about 2 seconds, then signal for the **t** sound.

The signal for say-it-fast is a hand drop. Step 4, Say it fast, should follow quickly after step 3.

Corrections. If students pause between the sounds in steps 2 and 3, follow this procedure. Say Don't stop between the sounds. Then repeat step 1, holding each sound for a shorter time—about half a second. ēēēt. Present steps 2 and 3 with the shorter sounds. Then repeat steps 1 through 3, holding each sound for a longer time—2 seconds. Remind students Don't stop between the sounds.

If students don't produce the second sound of the word the instant you hold up the second finger, tell them You must say each sound when I hold up a finger. Then repeat steps 1 through 3 until they are responding to the signal.

If some students fail to say it fast in step 4, follow this correction.

❶ You didn't say it fast.

❷ Call on a student who did say it fast and present steps 2 through 4 to that student. Say Listen to _____ say it fast.

❸ Present steps 2 through 4 to the student who made the say-it-fast error.

Word Reading

Lessons 1–65

The initial word-reading exercises involve sounding out each word and then saying the word fast. In Lesson 16, students are introduced to "reading the fast way." By this time the sounding out is done silently. Students simply study the word and then identify it without orally sounding it out.

Workbook Exercises provide students with practice in sounding out and reading words the fast way and with practice in analyzing word parts. Beginning with Lesson 22, parts of words are underlined. Students identify the underlined part and then read the entire word.

Irregular words are introduced in Lesson 47. Students learn that irregular words are spelled (or sounded out) one way but pronounced another way.

LESSON 1 Word Reading, Sounding Out Words

Task B   Me

1. Say each sound when I touch it.
   (Point to **m.**) What sound?
   (Touch under **m.**) *mmm.*
   (Point to **e.**) What sound?
   (Touch under **e.**) *ēēē.*
2. (Touch the ball of the arrow for **me.**)
   Now I'm going to sound out the word.
   I won't stop between the sounds.
   (Touch under **m, e** as you say:) **mmm**ēēē.
3. (Touch the ball of the arrow). Do it with me.
   Sound it out. Get ready.
   (Touch under **m, e.**) *mmm*ēēē. (Repeat until
   the students say the sounds without pausing.)
4. Again. Sound it out. Get ready.
   (Touch under **m, e.**) *mmm*ēēē.
   (Repeat until firm.)
5. All by yourselves. Sound it out. Get ready.
   (Touch under **m, e.**) *mmm*ēēē.
   (Repeat until firm.)
6. (Touch the ball of the arrow.) Say it fast.
   (Slash right, along the arrow.) *Me.* Yes, you
   read the word **me.**

Teaching Techniques. In step 1 students identify the component sounds of the word. You model the sounding out of the word in step 2. In steps 3 and 4 you lead students in sounding out the word. In step 5 they sound out the word without assistance. Finally, in step 6 they say the word fast.

The signal in step 6 of the format is the same one used in the rhyming tasks. Touch the ball of the arrow. Say Say it fast. Pause 1 second. Quickly move your finger to the right along the arrow. As soon as your finger moves, students should say the word fast.

Here's how to execute the signal to sound out the word.

❶ Touch the ball of the arrow as you say Sound it out. Get ready.

❷ Pause 1 second.

❸ Quickly loop your finger to a point just under the first sound of the word.

❹ Hold your finger there for 2 seconds (if the sound is continuous). Students should respond as soon as you touch under the sound, and continue saying the sound as long as you touch under it.

❺ Quickly loop to the next sound and hold for 2 seconds (if the sound is continuous). As soon as you touch under it, students should say this sound without pausing between the sounds.

❻ Quickly remove your finger from the page. The diagram on page 30 shows the pointing, looping, and student response.

Practice the signal for sounding out words before presenting word reading. You must loop very quickly from sound to sound. If you loop slowly, students may come in at different times or stop between the sounds.

Student response: **mmmmmmmeeeeeeee**

Note: To loop for double **e** in words such as **eem,** touch between the **e**'s, then under the **m.** For other letter combinations (**th, sh, ck,** etc.), touch between the two letters.

Corrections. If students misidentify a sound in step 1, say the correct sound as soon as you hear the error. Repeat step 1 until students are responding correctly to both sounds.

If students stop between the sounds in steps 3 through 5, follow this correction procedure.

❶ Say Don't stop between the sounds.

❷ Present steps 2 through 4, holding each sound for about half a second.

❸ Repeat steps 2 through 4, holding each sound for a longer period of time—about 2 seconds per sound.

❹ Repeat steps 3 through 5 until all the students are performing on each step.

If students fail to say the word fast in step 6, say the word fast and then repeat steps 3 through 6 until students are firm.

Several word-reading exercises follow the initial one. They are simple variations of the basic procedure—they involve fewer steps. The model and lead steps are dropped. The most abbreviated word-reading format involving sounding out begins in Lesson 10. Basically, it is steps 4 through 6 of the initial format. Students are directed to sound out and identify the word (say it fast).

By Lesson 16, students have practiced reading a variety of words, including some that contain stop sounds. The looping signal for words with stop sounds is similar to the one used for words composed of continuous sounds, except that you point under the stop sound for only an instant. If the stop sound appears at the end of the word, touch it as if it were hot—just for an instant. Then lift your finger from the page. If the stop sound occurs at the beginning of the word, loop from the ball of the arrow to the stop sound. Then, without pausing, continue to loop to the next sound. Your timing for these words must be precise. Say Get ready. Pause 1 second. Loop to the first and second letters of the word.

LESSON 16 Word Reading the Fast Way

In Lesson 16 students are taught to read words the fast way.

Task C   Word Reading the Fast Way

1. You're going to read these words the fast way. When you read the fast way, just tell me the word. You can sound it out to yourself, but not out loud.

2. (Touch the ball of the arrow for **me**. Pause 4 seconds.) What word? (Slash right.) *Me.*

3. (Touch the ball for **she**. Pause 4 seconds.) What word? (Slash right.) *She.*

4. (Touch the ball for **ran**. Pause 4 seconds.) What word? (Slash right.) *Ran.*

To correct:

a. (Say the correct word.)

b. What word? (Slash right.)

c. Sound it out. Get ready. (Touch under each sound as the students say the sounds without pausing.)

d. What word? (Slash right.) Yes, _____. Remember that word.

e. (Return to the first word in the list and present all the words in order.)

me

she

ran

Teaching Techniques. Present this format carefully. Some students will be unable to identify the word without sounding it out. If they are rushed or if you do not prompt them to figure out the word, they will revert to guessing.

Observe the students when you present steps 2 through 4. Look at their eyes and lips. If they simply stare at the word, chances are they won't identify it. If they move their eyes from sound to sound and perhaps move their lips, they probably will figure out the word correctly.

The 4-second pause is only a general rule; you should gauge the length of the pause by students' performance. You can do this by selecting one of the slower performers and saying Let me know when you're ready. If you rush students, they will probably develop guessing strategies.

The signal used to direct the reading is a slash along the arrow. Say What word? Pause 1 second. Then quickly slash right. Students should respond the moment your finger moves.

Early word-reading exercises have short word lists. As the program progresses, the number of words in the Word-Attack Exercises increases. These lists are screened into smaller more manageable lists of 4 to 7 words. Some lessons contain up to four word lists on a page. Repeat each list until firm before moving to the next list.

Individual Tests for Word Reading. The word-reading format does not indicate individual turns; however, they are important because they provide you with specific information about the performance of individual students. Give individual turns after the group has read all the specified words. Have individual students read at least two or three words in the exercise. A good practice is to call on lower-performing students. Point to the words you want them to read, but don't present words in the same sequence in which they appear in the format.

LESSON 47 Irregular Words

The irregular words taught are **was, said, to, what, you, do,** and **of.** Following is the basic irregular-word format.

=== **EXERCISE 3** ===

● **IRREGULAR WORD**

1. (Touch the ball of the arrow for **was.**)
   Sound out this word. Get ready. (Touch under **w, a, s.**) *wwwăăăsss. (Repeat until the students say the sounds without pausing.)*
2. That's how we sound out the word. But here's how we say the word: **wuz.** It's a funny word. How do we say the word? (Signal.) *Wuz.*
3. Sound it out. Get ready. (Touch under **w, a, s.**) *wwwăăăsss. (Repeat until firm.)*
4. Everybody, say the word. (Signal.) *Wuz.* Yes, **wuz.** Remember that word.

Teaching Techniques. In step 1 students sound out the word. In step 2 tell them how to *say* the word. In steps 3 and 4 test them on sounding out and saying the word.

In steps 1 and 3 make sure students say the sounds on the page. They should not identify the **a** sound as "ŭŭŭ" or the **s** sound as "zzz." Low-performing readers frequently have serious misunderstandings about irregular words and can become more confused if you allow them to sound out "wŭz" in steps 1 and 3.

Steps 3 and 4 may have to be repeated in sequence several times. Do not consider students firm on this exercise until they can respond to these steps without error.

Corrections. There are two basic mistakes students make in the irregular-words exercises.

To correct distorted sounding out, particularly in steps 1 and 3, point to each "irregular" letter in the word (**a** and **s**). Ask What sound? . . . So what are you going to say for this letter when we sound out the word? Then say Sound out the word.

Remember to say the sounds that are written. Repeat the sounding out until students are firm.

Some students, when asked to say the word, will pronounce it as if it were a regular word—for example, they'll pronounce **was** as if it rhymed with **glass.** To correct students who mispronounce the word in step 4, tell them You didn't say the word. Here's how we say the word: **wuz.** How do we say the word? Stress the word **say.** Then repeat steps 3 and 4, stressing the instructions: Sound it out . . . Say the word.

If students have chronic problems with steps 3 and 4, lead them through both steps, presenting the instructions as indicated previously. Then test them on steps 3 and 4 in sequence.

Students should be firmed on each irregular word when it is presented. In the lesson following the introduction of an irregular word, there is a format that tests students on sounding out and saying the word. Generally, this testing format is repeated for at least eight more lessons.

Workbook Exercises

The second part of each lesson is devoted to the individual student Workbook lessons. The first four Workbook lessons are one-page lessons; the rest are two-page lessons.

The number of exercises in a Workbook lesson ranges from five to eight. This list of Workbook Exercises shows the lessons where each appears.

Exercise	Lesson
Sound dictation	1–65
Sound it out	1–4
Matching sounds	1–8
Matching and copying sounds	1–11
Matching completion	9–65
Circle game	1–65
Word reading	5–65
Word copying	6–25
Word completion	6–65
Sentence reading	18–29
Spelling from dictation	26–65
Story reading	30–65

The major skills associated with word reading—blending, sounding out, and reading the fast way—are introduced in the teacher-directed Word-Attack Exercises—not in the Workbook pages. After a few lessons of teacher presentation, however, Workbook exercises that involve the newly taught skill begin to appear.

Some ancillary skills do appear in the Workbook pages without any previous teacher presentation. These include matching sounds, matching and copying sounds, and the circle game.

Sound Dictation

Lessons 1–65

Following the introduction of each new sound, students write that sound on their Workbook pages. For example, in Lesson 1 the sounds **m, a, s, e,** and **t** are introduced. Then, in the same lesson, these sounds are used in a Workbook sound-dictation exercise.

LESSON 1 Sound Dictation with Display

================ EXERCISE 6 ================

● **SOUND DICTATION**

1. Everybody, touch part 1 in your Workbook.
   ✔ These are the sounds you did before. Say all the sounds once more before you write the letters.
2. Touch the first sound. ✔ What sound? (Clap.) *t.* Yes, **t.**
3. Touch the next sound. ✔ What sound? (Clap.) *ăăă.* Yes, **ăăă.**
4. (Repeat step 3 for **sss, ēēē, mmm.**)
5. Now you're going to write the letters for the sounds I say. First sound. (Pause.) **mmm.** What sound? (Clap.) *mmm.* Write it in the first blank. (Check work and correct.)
6. Next sound. (Pause.) *ēēē.* What sound? (Clap.) *ēēē.* Write it in the next blank. (Check work and correct.)
7. (Repeat step 6 for **t, ăăă, sss, ēēē, mmm, t, sss, ăăă.**)
8. (Check that students can write all the letters without errors.)

   t   a   s   e   m

___ ___ ___ ___ ___ ___ ___ ___ ___

Teaching Techniques. A clap signals students to say the sound when you ask What sound?

In steps 5 through 7 you say a sound, such as **mmm.** Ask the students What sound? Then tell them to write it. They should write a single letter for each instruction—not **mmm,** for example. The **mmm** in the format merely signifies that when you say the sound, you hold it for about 2 seconds.

For this format, do not allow students to write sounds before you signal Write it. Make sure all students respond clearly to What sound? In this way, you can tell if anyone did not hear the sound correctly.

Monitor the performance of students as you present the sounds. Make sure that (a) students do not copy from each other, and (b) they write the correct letter for each sound you dictate. Circulate among students as you present the activity; don't just stand in front of the group.

Corrections. Note every mistake students make, and correct the mistakes immediately.

For writing mistakes, tell the student You wrote the right sound, but you wrote it backwards. Cross out the **sss** you have written. Look at the book and copy it the right way. Then repeat that sound after all specified sounds have been dictated. For example, if you note that some students have made mistakes on the sounds **sss** and **ēēē,** repeat them at the end of the list.

LESSON 8 Sound Dictation (no display)

After Lesson 7, students no longer see a sound display in the Workbook. Correct their writing mistakes by printing the letter on the board. The students who make the error should cross out what they have written and copy the correct letter next to it. Also, continue to add the missed sounds to the end of the sound-dictation list.

LESSON 9 Sound Combinations

Beginning in Lesson 9, some sound combinations are introduced in sound-dictation exercises. Also beginning in Lesson 9, students will receive points for their sound-dictation performance. Before points are awarded, make sure students draw a line through any missed sound (including those that are written improperly). Then have them write it correctly next to the missed sound.

Lessons 5–65

The introduction of Workbook word-reading exercises is preceded by activities that involve sounding out words and reading words from the teacher's book. In word reading, students (a) touch under the first letter of a word and say the sound, and (b) quickly move their fingers under the remaining letters and say the sounds without stopping.

LESSON 5 Word Reading: Workbook

━━━━━━━━━ **EXERCISE 8** ━━━━━━━━━

● **WORD READING: Workbook**

1. Everybody, touch word one in part 2. ✔
2. Sound it out. Get ready. (Clap for each sound as the students touch under **a, d.**) *ăăăd.*
   (Repeat until the students say the sounds without pausing.)
   To correct sound errors:
   a. (Say the correct sound loudly as soon as you hear an error.)
   b. Everybody, touch the sound ____ . What sound? (Signal.)
   c. (Repeat step 2.)
3. Again. Sound it out. Get ready. (Clap for each sound.) *ăăăd.* Say it fast. (Signal.) *Ad.* Yes, **ad.**
   To correct errors:
   a. (Say the correct word:) **ad.**
   b. What word? (Signal.) *Ad.*
   c. You're going to sound it out again. Get ready. (Clap for each sound.) *ăăăd.*
   d. Say it fast. (Signal.) *Ad.*
   e. (Go to the next word.)
4. Touch word two. ✔
5. Sound it out. Get ready. (Clap for each sound as the students touch under **a, t.**) *ăăăt.*
   (Repeat until the students say the sounds without pausing.)
6. Again. Sound it out. Get ready. (Clap for each sound.) *ăăăt.* Say it fast. (Signal.) *At.* Yes, **at.**
7. (Repeat steps 4–6 for **sat, sad, mad, rat, eem, reem, am, ram, sam.**)

Teaching Techniques. In step 2 say Sound it out. Get ready. Pause for 1 second. Then clap for the sound **ăăă.** Students should point under **a** and say the sound. They keep saying **ăăă** for about 2 seconds, until you clap for **d.** Responding to the second clap, they move their finger to the **d** and complete the word: **ăăăd.**

In step 3 you also say Say it fast. Pause 1 second and clap. Students should say the word fast: **ad.**

The procedure is repeated for each word that appears in part 2 in the Workbook pages.

Corrections. When students do not point under the appropriate letters, prompt them by moving their fingers under the appropriate letters. Then repeat the word until they can perform without any prompting from you.

Follow these steps to correct sound-identification errors.

❶ Say the correct sound as soon as you hear a mistake. For example, say **ăăă.**

❷ Everybody, touch the sound **ăăă.** What sound? Signal.

❸ Sound out the word again. Get ready. Clap for each sound.

If students make a mistake on any word in a row, first correct the error; then return to the first word in the row and repeat all the words in sequence. When students can respond correctly to all the words in a row, proceed to the next row.

LESSON 17 Reading the Fast Way

The general procedures are similar to those specified for sounding out words, except that students say the word in response to one clap. Say What word? Pause 1 second and clap. Students say the word at a normal rate.

When you say What word? or Next word, students should touch under the appropriate word. Make sure they are looking at the right word. Remind them to figure out the word.

Follow the corrections specified in the exercise.

LESSON 25 Word Part, Whole Word

In this format, students read part of the word and then the entire word. The part of the word to be read first is underlined.

======== EXERCISE 7 ========

- **WORD READING: Workbook**
1. Touch the first word in part 3. ✔ Tell me the sound for the underlined part. Then tell me the word.
2. Touch the underlined sound in the first word. *(Pause.)* What sound? (Signal.) *sss.* (Pause.) What word? (Signal.) *Cats.*
3. Touch the underlined sound in the next word. (Pause.) What sound? (Signal.) *sss.* (Pause.) What word? (Signal.) *Sheets.*
4. (Repeat step 3 for remaining words.)

Corrections. The major mistake that students make is identifying the entire word when they are being asked to identify only part of it. Tell them what they are doing. You're telling me the word. But I didn't say: What word? I said: What sound? Tell me the sound. Stress the instructions when presenting the task. What sound? . . . What word?

Word Completion

Lessons 6–65

The word-completion activities are closely coordinated with the pronunciation activities. In pronunciation exercises, students learn to identify the first sound, middle sound, and last sound of three-sound words. In the first type of the word-completion exercises, students create words that rhyme with words (or parts) printed on the Workbook pages. The word created rhymes with the printed word. In later activities starting at Lesson 21, students first write a word, then add an initial sound to create a word that rhymes.

Beginning with Lesson 19, students also create words that alliterate. Word beginnings appear in the Workbook pages. Students are directed to change the words by adding specified ending sounds.

LESSON 6 Word Completion

In the first word-completion exercise, the students sound out the word part **at.** Then they change **at** to say **mat** (steps 4 and 5). In steps 7–10, the procedure is repeated, with the students changing **at** to **sat.**

═══════ EXERCISE 7 ═══════

● **WORD COMPLETION**

1. Everybody, touch the first word in part 2. ✔
2. Sound it out. Get ready. (Clap for each sound as the students touch under **a, t.**) *aat.* (Repeat until the students say the sounds without pausing.)
3. Say it fast. (Signal.) *At.* Yes, **at.**
4. You're going to change **at** to say (pause) **mat.** What will it say? (Signal.) *Mat.*
5. The first sound in mat is **mmm.** What sound? (Signal.) *mmm.* Write the letter for **mmm** before (pause) **at.** (Check work and correct.)
6. You started with the word (pause) **at.** Now you have the word **mat.** What word did you start with? (Signal.) *At.* Yes, **at.**
   And what word do you have now? (Signal.) *Mat.* Yes, **mat.**
7. Touch the word on the next arrow. ✔ That word says (pause) **at.**
8. You're going to change **at** to say (pause) **sat.** What will it say? (Signal.) *Sat.*
9. The first sound in **sat** is **sss.** So, what do you write before (pause) **at?** (Signal.) *sss.* Yes, **sss.** Do it. (Check work and correct.)
10. You started with the word (pause) **at.** What word do you have now? (Signal.) *Sat.* Yes, **sat.**

Teaching Techniques. If students are firm on sounding out the other exercises presented in Lessons 1 through 5 (such as sound dictation), they should have little trouble with this activity. However, you should hold them to a very firm criterion on the early word-completion exercises. They teach students the relationship between a change in the structure of a word (adding a beginning letter) and the sound of the word (creating a word that rhymes).

LESSON 19 Word Completion

In this format, the students learn to add a letter (or letters) to the end of a word part.

═══════ EXERCISE 9 ═══════

● **WORD COMPLETION**

1. Everybody, touch part 6. ✔
2. Sound out the word on the first arrow. Get ready. (Clap for **m, a.**) *mmmăăă.* What word? (Signal.) *Ma.* Yes, **ma.**
3. Fix it up to say (pause) **mad.** (Pause.) **Mad.** What word? (Signal.) *Mad.* Yes, **mad.** Fix it up. (Check work and correct.)
4. Sound out the word on the next arrow. Get ready. (Clap for **m, a.**) *mmmăăă.* What word? (Signal.) *Ma.* Yes, **ma.**
5. Fix it up to say (pause) **mat.** (Pause.) **Mat.** What word? (Signal.) *Mat.* Yes, **mat.** Fix it up. (Check work and correct.)
6. Sound out the word on the next arrow. Get ready. (Clap for **c, a.**) *căăă.* What word? (Signal.) *Ca.* Yes, **ca.**
7. Fix it up to say (pause) **cat.** (Pause.) **Cat.** What word? (Signal.) *Cat.* Yes, **cat.** Fix it up. (Check work and correct.)
8. Sound out the word on the next arrow. Get ready. (Clap for **c, a.**) *căăă.* What word? (Signal.) *Ca.* Yes, **ca.**
9. Fix it up to say (pause) **can.** (Pause.) **Can.** What word? (Signal.) *Can.* Yes, **can.** Fix it up. (Check work and correct.)

Teaching Techniques. Listen carefully to the student responses in step 2. Frequently, students add endings. If in doubt, call on individual students to identify the word.

Corrections. If students have trouble figuring out where to write the letter **d,** follow this correction.

❶ I'll say the sounds. You touch them. **mmmăăă.**

❷ Let's do it again. This time, show me where the new sound will go. **mmmăăă.** Repeat step 2 until the students are firm.

❸ Repeat steps 2 and 3 of the format.

LESSON 27 Advanced Word Completion

In Lessons 27 through 31, the word-completion exercises concentrate on adding ending sounds to words. For example, students will be instructed to fix up the letters **ca** to say **cats.** A common mistake they make is to omit one of the sounds—writing **cas,** for example.

To correct these mistakes, follow this procedure.

❶ Tell the students Here's how you write **cats.** First write **cat.** Then write the last sound in **cats.**

❷ Write **cat.** ✔

❸ Now add the last sound in **catsss.**

If students continue to make this type of mistake, require them to repeat the words they misspelled.

Spelling from Dictation

Lessons 26–65

Before spelling is introduced in Lesson 26, students practice word-copying on their daily Workbook pages.

The spelling activities are closely linked with other activities in the program. Beginning in

Lesson 6, students copy words that are written on their Workbook pages. These are words that students read earlier in the lesson. The word-completion exercises provide students with practice in adding beginning sounds and ending sounds to words or word parts.

For the spelling-dictation format, you say a word **(cat),** then say it slowly **(căăăt).** Students write the word.

LESSON 26 Spelling from Dictation

═══════ **EXERCISE 5** ═══════

● **SPELLING FROM DICTATION**

1. Touch part 1 in your Workbook. ✔ This spelling exercise is worth 2 points. You're going to write words in the blanks as I dictate them.

2. First word: **cat.** What word? (Signal.) *Cat.* **Cat** has three sounds. I'll say **cat** a sound at a time. Listen: **c . . . ăăă . . . t.** Listen again: **c . . . ăăă . . . t.**

3. Your turn. Say the sounds in **cat.** Get ready. (Clap three times.) *c . . . ăăă . . . t.*

4. Write the word **cat** in the first blank. (Check work and correct.)

   To correct:
   a. Say the sounds in **cat.** Get ready.
   b. Show me the letter for **c.** (Check and correct.) Show me the letter for **ăăă.** (Check and correct.) Show me the letter for **t.** (Check and correct.)

5. Next word: **did.** What word? (Signal.) *Did.* I'll say **did** a sound at a time. Listen: **d . . . ĭĭĭ . . . d.**

6. Your turn. Say the sounds in **did.** Get ready. (Clap three times.) *d . . . ĭĭĭ . . . d.*

7. Write the word **did** in the next blank. (Check work and correct.)

8. (Repeat steps 5–7 for **dad, she.**)

Corrections. If the students omit letters, prompt them with this procedure.

❶ Say I'll show you the sounds you have to write.

❷ Hold up a finger for each sound that you say. For the word **cat,** quickly hold up fingers as you say **c, ăăă,** and **t.**

❸ Require students who make mistakes to hold up fingers with you.

This procedure will prompt the number of sounds they are to write, but it will not always indicate the number of letters in the word. For example, the sound **shsh** is composed of two letters, which students are taught to treat as a single sound.

If students write incorrect letters in words, follow the correction procedure specified in the format. You can also use the correction procedure if letters are omitted.

When students make an error, have them cross out the word and write the correct word next to it. If someone misses a word, do not award that student any points for spelling dictation.

Sentence Reading

Lessons 18–29

The sentence-reading exercises give students practice in reading words that are presented within a context. Usually, students who qualify for this program do not understand what decoding is. This problem is magnified when they try to read sentences. Usually, their sentence-reading strategy involves guessing based on the syntax or the position of words within the sentence. For instance, the first word is typically called "the."

The objective of the sentence-reading activities is to retrain students in how they go about reading words in sentences. Although work on isolated words (in lists) teaches word-attack skills, work on reading sentences ensures that students apply these skills.

The sentences in this program are designed so that there is low probability of guessing a word correctly. If students guess the next word in a sentence on the basis of the preceding words, they will most likely be wrong. The low-probability feature provides students with consistent evidence that guessing is not effective. A guess equals a mistake; therefore, students quickly abandon the guessing approach and use the decoding skills being taught.

Here are the details of the sentence-reading activities, which are among the most important exercises in the program.

◆ Words in all sentences should be read the fast way.

◆ All sentences are composed of words that have been presented in word-attack and word-reading activities.

◆ Following the group reading of the sentences, individual students read the sentences.

◆ After students read each sentence, comprehension questions are presented.

LESSON 18 Sentence Reading

Following is the introductory sentence-reading presentation. Only one sentence is read.

EXERCISE 8

● **SENTENCE READING**

Task A

1. Everybody, touch part 5. ✔
2. This is a sentence. The first word of the sentence starts with a capital letter.
3. You're going to read each word in the sentence the fast way.
4. Touch under the first word. ✔
   What word? (Signal.) *She.*
5. Next word. (Students touch under the next word.) ✔ What word? (Signal.) *Had.*
6. Next word. (Students touch under the next word.) ✔ What word? (Signal.) *Rats.*
7. (Repeat step 6 for **and, cats.**)
   To correct word-reading errors:
   a. (Say the correct word.)
   b. What word? (Signal.)
   c. Everybody, back to the first word of the sentence.
   d. (Repeat steps 4–7.)
8. (Repeat steps 4–7 until the students correctly identify all the words in the sentence in order.)

Individual test

Everybody, point to the first word in the sentence. (Call on a student.) Take your time. See if you can read all the words in this sentence the fast way without making a mistake. Everybody else, touch under the words that are read. (Call on different students to read the sentence.)

Task B

1. Everybody, touch under the first word of the sentence. ✔
2. I'll read the sentence. Follow along.
   She had rats and cats.
3. Here are some questions:
   a. What did she have? (Signal.)
      Rats and cats.
   b. Who had those rats and cats? (Signal.)
      She did.

Teaching Techniques. Students read the sentence in unison. After they read a word, say Next word. This signals students to touch under the next word. They must touch under the words they are reading. Say What word? Pause 1 second, and clap once. When you clap, they are to say the word.

After the group has read the sentence, present individual turns. When a student is reading, the other students should be pointing under the words as they are read.

Errors will be minimized on sentence-reading activities if you follow these procedures.

◆ Make sure students look at the word. They should not look at you. If they do, point to the word and show them where they are to look.

◆ Pause before asking What word? If you do not pause, some students will guess or not respond. Pause longer before words that have been missed in the past. Also, caution students:

This word is hard. Figure it out. Students may have particular trouble with:

❶ Words that begin with two consonants **(sl, sp, cl, dr, tr)**

❷ Words that begin with sound combinations **(wh, th, sh, ch)**

❸ Words that end in two consonants **(nd, nt, it, mp,** and so on)

❹ Words that end with **s, ing, er,** and **y**

❺ Irregularly spelled words **(what, said, was, to, you,** and so on)

◆ Say the word after students have read it. Some students in the group may have responded incorrectly, but you may not have heard them. If you get in the habit of quickly saying the correct word after each word is read, you reduce the risk of having the wrong word reinforced.

◆ Require students to say the words clearly. If you are not absolutely certain what they are saying, ask them. They could be mumbling because they don't know the word.

◆ Reinforce students for hard work. Reassure them that the sentences are hard and that they are working well.

Corrections. Follow these procedures for correcting mistakes.

❶ Treat any mispronunciation or nonresponse as an error.

❷ Say the correct word as soon as you hear an error.

❸ Instruct students Sound it out. Get ready. Pause 1 second and clap for each sound in the word. Repeat the sounding out until the responses are firm. Then ask What word?

❹ Tell the students Go back to the first word of the sentence. Check to make sure they are touching under the first word. Pause. Say Get ready. Clap for the word. Continue with the remaining words in the sentence.

❺ Before asking them to identify the word they missed, remind them This is that tough word. Allow an adequate pause before saying What word?

❻ Correct mistakes until they read the entire sentence without an error.

If students do not point to the words that are being read, tell or show them what to do.

If a student makes a mistake on an individual turn, follow the correction procedure described above. Say the correct

word. Then have the student sound out the word, identify the word, and read the sentence from the beginning. Just before the student rereads the missed word, say This is that tough word.

Story Reading

Lesson 30–65

For Lessons 30 through 42, the stories that students read are illustrated. For the remainder of the program, the stories are not illustrated.

LESSON 30 Story Reading

The story reading procedure involves two parts. The first part is decoding (Task A). The second part is comprehension (Task B). When decoding the story, students read a word at a time. Then you re-read the story and ask comprehension questions.

═══════ EXERCISE 11 ═══════

● **STORY READING**

Task A

1. Everybody, touch part 7. ✔
2. This is a story. There are pictures after some of the sentences. You're going to read the sentences the fast way.
3. Touch under the first word. ✔
   What word? (Signal.) *She.*
4. Next word. ✔ What word? (Signal.) *Had.*
5. (Repeat step 4 for **3 fish.**)
   To correct word-reading errors:
   a. (Say the correct word.)
   b. What word? (Signal.)
   c. Everybody, back to the first word of the sentence. ✔
   d. (Repeat steps 3–5.)
6. (Repeat steps 3–5 for each remaining sentence. **This fish is a shad.**
   This fish is a cod.
   This fish is in the cat.)

7. (If students miss more than 4 words, repeat the story reading from the beginning.)

Task B

1. Now I'll read the story and ask questions. Follow along.
2. **She had three fish.** Everybody, how many fish did she have? (Signal.) *Three.*
3. **This fish is a shad.** Touch the picture of the shad. ✔
4. **This fish is a cod.** Touch the picture of the cod. ✔
5. **This fish is in the cat.** I don't see the fish. Where is it?
   (Call on a student.) *In the cat.*
   (Call on a student.) How did it get in the cat? Idea: The cat ate it.
   (Call on a student.) Why does the cat look happy? (Accept a reasonable response.)

Teaching Techniques. The story-reading procedures are the same as those used for sentence reading. Make sure that students are able to read an entire sentence before going on to the next. If students make more than 4 errors before completing the story, return to the beginning of the story and repeat it.

Corrections. Follow the correction procedure specified in the format. Say the correct word, ask what the word is, direct students to return to the beginning of the sentence in which the mistake occurred, and repeat the reading of the sentence.

Related Skills

LESSONS 48–65 Whole-Sentence Reading

Beginning in Lesson 48, you direct sentence reading "the fast way." You simply clap for each word without first saying Next word. . . . What word?. . . .

This format introduces the sentence-reading procedure.

═══════ **EXERCISE 9** ═══════

● **SENTENCE READING**
1. Everybody, touch part 5. ✔
2. I'm going to read all the words in sentence 1 the fast way. I'll clap and read a word each time I clap. Here I go. (Clap for each word. Pause about 2 seconds between claps as you read:) The . . . black . . . colt . . . will . . . trot . . . on . . . the . . . track.
3. Your turn to read sentence 1 the fast way. Read a word each time I clap.
4. Touch under the first word. ✔ Get ready. (Clap for each word. Pause about 2 seconds between claps.) *The . . . black . . . colt . . . will . . . trot . . . on . . . the . . . track.*
5. (Repeat step 4 until the students correctly identify all the words in the sentence in order.)
6. Touch under the first word of sentence 2. ✔ Get ready. (Clap for each word. Pause about 2 seconds between claps.) *Her . . . hat . . . fits . . . but . . . her . . . wig . . . is . . . big.*
7. (Repeat step 6 until the students read the sentence without a mistake.)
8. (Repeat steps 6 and 7 for each remaining sentence.)

Individual test
(Give each student a chance to read one of the sentences. Praise students who read accurately without long pauses.)

LESSONS 53–65 Quotation Marks

In Lesson 53 students are introduced to sentences that have quotation marks. Students learn to discriminate between the whole sentence and the part of the sentence that a person said.

The format below is from Lesson 54, the second lesson in which quotation mark exercises appear.

EXERCISE 8

- **SENTENCE READING: Quotations**
1. Everybody, touch sentence 1 in part 4. ✔
2. Read the sentence. Get ready.
   (Clap for each word. Pause about 2 seconds between claps.) *He . . . said, . . . "I . . . will . . . win . . . the . . . meet."*
3. I'll say the whole sentence. **He said, "I will win the meet."**
4. (Call on a student.) Say the words he said.
   I will win the meet.
5. Everybody, touch sentence 2. ✔
   Read the sentence. Get ready. (Clap for each word. Pause about 2 seconds between claps.) *She . . . said, . . . "Fix . . . the . . . casters . . . on . . . that . . . bed."*
6. I'll say the whole sentence. **She said, "Fix the casters on that bed."**
7. (Call on a student.) Say the words she said.
   Fix the casters on that bed.
8. Everybody, touch sentence 3. ✔ Read the sentence. Get ready. (Clap for each word.)
   The . . . clock . . . was . . . running . . . faster.
9. (Repeat step 8 for each remaining sentence.)

Support Activities

The following Workbook Exercises support the basic program goal of teaching a consistent decoding strategy: matching sounds, matching and copying sounds, matching completion, and the circle game.

Matching Sounds

Lessons 1–8

The matching-sounds exercises present two columns of letters. After identifying the sounds, students draw lines from the letters in the first column to the corresponding letters in the second column.

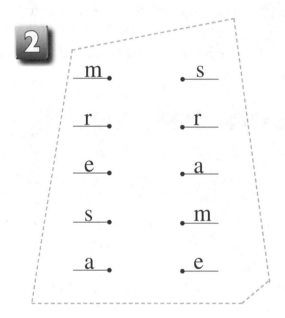

Matching and Copying Sounds

Lessons 1–11

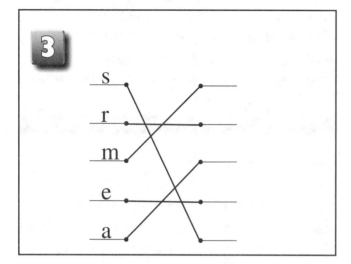

These exercises present a column of sounds and a column of blanks. A line connects each letter in the first column to a blank in the second column. Students follow the line from a letter and write that letter in the second column.

Matching Completion

Lessons 9–65

Next to a column of words is a second column displaying part of each word from the first column. In Lessons 9 through 46, lines connect each word to its incomplete counterpart. Students match and complete the words independently. After Lesson 46, students also draw the connecting lines.

This is the format that introduces the first matching-completion exercise.

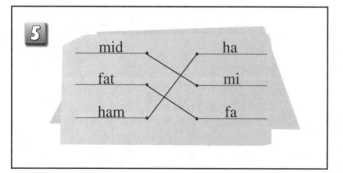

- **MATCHING COMPLETION**

Task A Mid

1. Everybody, touch part 5. ✔ This is a new type of matching exercise. The words are written in the first column. A sound is missing from each word in the second column.
2. Touch the top word in the first column. ✔ Sound it out. Get ready. (Clap for **m, i, d.**) *mmmiiid.* What word? (Signal.) *Mid.*
3. Touch the next word in the first column. ✔ Sound it out. Get ready. (Clap for **f, a, t.**) *fffăăăt.* What word? (Signal.) *Fat.*
4. (Repeat step 3 for **ham.**)
5. Touch the top word in the first column. ✔ That word is **mid.** Follow the line to the word in the second column. ✔
6. Sound out that word. Get ready. (Clap for **m, i.**) *mmmiii.* (Repeat until the students say the sounds without pausing.)
7. Does that word say **mid?** (Signal.) *No.*
8. *What sound is missing?* (Signal.) *d.* Yes, **d.**
   To correct:
   a. (Hold up the Workbook page. Point to **d** in **mid.**) Here's the sound that is missing. What sound? (Signal.) *d.*
   b. (Repeat steps 5–8 until firm.)
9. Write in the letter for the missing sound. (Check work and correct.)

The matching-completion exercises reinforce spelling and decoding skills. They also help set the stage for reading the fast way, because each word is referred to as a unit after it is identified (steps 5 through 7 of the format).

Teaching Techniques. This format should be presented quite quickly. The only place students may have trouble is in step 8, where they are asked to identify the missing sound.

Corrections. Follow the correction procedure specified in the format for mistakes at step 8. Practice this correction before presenting the activity. For word-reading mistakes, use the correction procedures specified earlier in this guide.

Circle Game

Lessons 1–65

In the first 32 Workbook lessons, students practice discriminating between letters. At the left end of each double row is a circled letter or letter combination. The circled symbol indicates what the students should circle in these two rows. If the letter **r** appears to the left, students are to circle every **r** in those two rows.

A variation of the circle game is introduced in Lesson 33. Students now circle words that are printed with no spacing between them.

The circle game provides practice in discriminating between letters. The exercise focuses attention on details, a very important skill for the poor reader. The initial activities are not difficult. However, when sound

combinations **(sh, th, wh)** are introduced, students frequently have trouble identifying all the examples that appear in a row.

Following are the student material and the teacher-presentation format for the circle game that appear in Lesson 10.

Note that students do the circle game and some other Workbook Exercises independently. In Lesson 10 this independent work includes matching and copying sounds. Earlier, these activities had been directed by the teacher.

══════ EXERCISE 12 ══════

CIRCLE GAME
1. Everybody, touch part 7 in your Workbook. ✔
2. What will you circle in the first two lines? (Signal.) *ththth.*
3. What will you circle in the next two lines? (Signal.) *h.*
4. What will you circle in the last two lines? (Signal.) *t.*
5. Circle the sounds and finish the rest of your Workbook lesson.

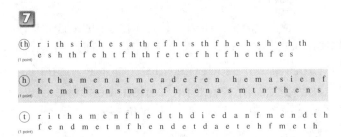

Individual Reading Checkouts

The Individual Reading Checkouts require about 3 minutes for each student. For groups of four or more, you will probably need someone else to help you check.

The following have been used as checkers: participants in work-study programs, high school students working on special projects, high-performing students in the school who are assigned to study periods, classroom aides, and sometimes the best-performing students in the group.

If you use students in the group as checkers, you should check them first at the beginning of the checkout period. Then assign specific students for them to check out.

Checkers need to be familiar with procedures for checking and recording. A checker should follow these procedures.

1 Sit next to the student, preferably at a table.

2 If the student must finish reading within a certain time, use a stopwatch or the classroom clock. Tell the student when to begin.

3 If the student misidentifies a word, immediately say the word correctly. If the student misidentifies a sound when sounding out the word—for example, saying "mmmēēē" for the word **ma**—immediately point to the **a** and say ăăă.

4 Circle the word in which a mistake occurs. In the example above, you would circle the word **ma.**

5 If the student is unable to figure out a word after 5 seconds, give the correct response and circle the word that was not identified.

6 After the student has read the material, add the number of circled words to determine the student's points.

7 If a time limit is specified for the checkout (Lessons 46 through 65), determine whether the student has read the material within the time limit. If not, tell the student You did not earn any points, but you can study some more and read the sentences again. If you read them within the time limit, you can still earn points.

In order for students completing **Decoding A** to be prepared for the beginning of **Decoding B1,** they must be able to read with fair accuracy at the rate of 60 words per minute by the end of **Decoding A.** The reading rates during the Individual Reading Checkouts progress from 45 words per minute at Lesson 46 to 60 words per minute at Lesson 65.

Place strong emphasis on the Individual Reading Checkouts near the end of the program. If students have trouble meeting rate-accuracy criteria, repeat Lessons 50 through 65. Note that the In–Program Mastery Tests for **Decoding A** indicate review procedures for groups that fail to meet rate criteria on Individual Reading Checkouts.

Do not make repeating lessons seem like punishment. You came close. You just need a little more practice. If students show signs of becoming nervous, remind them to Take it easy during Individual Reading Checkouts. The simplest cure for nervousness is more successful practice.

Awarding and Recording Points

Awarding Points

Points are awarded three times during each period.

Group points are awarded after the presentation of Word-Attack exercises. Pass out the Workbooks and then tell the group how many points were earned. Say either Everybody worked hard in the word-attack part so everybody gets 4 points for word attack or Not everybody worked very well during this part of the lesson, so nobody gets points for word attack today. But everybody will get a chance to earn points on the Workbook pages.

Individual points are awarded after students do their Workbook pages and after the reading checkout. Criterion information for awarding Workbook pages points and checkout points appears in each lesson.

Workbook Points. The number of points students can earn for specific Workbook exercises is indicated in parentheses below those activities. If "1 point" is below an activity, a student can earn either 0 or 1 point for that activity.

The teacher's script provides directions for point-earning activities. For example, the following appears in Lesson 4.

1. Everybody, touch part 3. ✔ At the bottom of the sound-matching box, it tells how many points you can earn for this exercise. Ask a student How many points can you earn? *1 point* Then say If you match all the sounds correctly, you earn 1 point. You're going to draw lines to match the letters. Get ready to say the sounds in the first column.

After the Workbook exercises have been completed, instructions for awarding Workbook points appears in the script.

════════ **EXERCISE 13** ════════

• **WORKBOOK CHECK**

> **Note: See the Teacher's Guide for Workbook correction procedures.**

1. (Check each student's Workbook.)
2. (Award points for matching sounds, matching and copying sounds, and the circle game.)
3. (Circle "1 point" below each activity in which a point was earned.)
4. (Write the student's total points in Box B. Maximum = 5 points.)

Check each student's Workbook pages as soon as the work has been completed. The student must get all parts of an activity correct to earn a point for the activity. This criterion applies to all Workbook exercises.

Reading-Checkout Points. In Lessons 1 through 4, students earn individual checkout points for sounding out words that appear in the Workbook pages. In Lessons 5 through 22, they earn points for reading a group of words. In Lessons 23 through 29, they read sentences; and in Lessons 30 through 45, they read stories. Beginning with Lesson 46 and continuing through the end of the program, students earn points by reading a story within a specified time limit.

For the checkout, students are to read individually to you, to an aide, or to a student who can reliably identify errors in reading. Points are awarded on the basis of accuracy (Lessons 1 through 45) or a combination of accuracy and rate (Lessons 46 through 65). The presentation material specifies the error limit and points for each checkout. For example, in Lessons 1 through 45, a student making more than 1 error earns no points. But a student who reads without errors or with only 1 error earns 4 points.

A student who does not earn any points on the Individual Reading Checkout can study the words or sentences again and request another checkout. If the second checkout is successful, the student earns the points specified for the checkout. If a student consistently fails the first checkout, you may want to impose a penalty—not awarding the full number of points for the second checkout. However, do not introduce this penalty before Lesson 8.

The Daily Point Chart

Here is a sample Point Chart. The chart appears at the top of every Workbook pages.

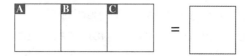

After completing the word-attack part of the lesson, tell the students how many points the group earned. Each student writes the number of points in Box A. For example, if the group earned 4 points for Word Attack Skills, all the students write **4** in Box A on their Workbook pages. If the group did not earn any points, they all write 0 in Box A.

After checking a student's independent Workbook exercises, total the points earned and write the number in Box B, or have the student write it.

After an Individual Reading Checkout, the checker enters the points in Box C. If the student did not earn any points and wants another checkout on the material, nothing

should be recorded. If the student is satisfied with the points earned, the checker records the number in Box C.

The total for the lesson is tabulated by adding the points in Boxes A, B, and C. Either the checker or the student can write the total in the last box.

The Point Summary Chart

On the inside front cover of the student's book is the Point Summary Chart, which is designed to show the student's point performance for each five-lesson block.

After the points have been awarded and recorded at the top of the Workbook pages, the student is to record the total number of points earned for the daily lesson in the appropriate box of the Point Summary Chart.

This is a sample of the Point Summary Chart filled in for the first fourteen lessons.

BLOCK 1		BLOCK 2		BLOCK 3	
Lesson	Points	Lesson	Points	Lesson	Points
1	4	6	8	11	9
2	6	7	9	12	6
3	6	8	8	13	10
4	9	9	7	14	13
5	8	10	10	15	
TOTAL	33	TOTAL	42	TOTAL	

As shown in the sample of the Point Summary Chart, the student has completed 14 lessons. After the next lesson, the student will enter the total number of points earned for Lesson 15, add the numbers for Lessons 11 through 15, and write the total for Block 3.

The Progress Graph

After totaling the points for each five-lesson block, the student is to plot that total on the Progress Graph on the inside back cover of the student's book. These are sample graphs filled in for the first two five-lesson blocks.

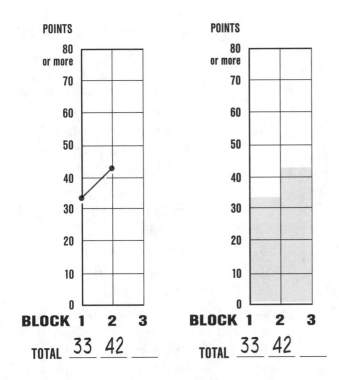

These records are important for two reasons. First, they show students their own progress. Second, they allow you to identify problems, reinforce students for good work, and figure grades for each grading period.

The In-Program Mastery Tests

The purpose of the Mastery Tests is to provide you with information about student performance and to indicate remedies for groups or students who have not mastered specific reading skills.

Mastery Tests are presented as part of each lesson specified in the list at right. The remedies for poor performance are specified in the right column. Note that the teacher-presentation script for the lesson contains complete details about the criterion of performance, the rate for sentence or story reading (if applicable), and the remedy for inadequate student performance.

Tests 1 through 5 are administered at the end of the specified lessons. Tests 6–12 are part of the lesson, the Individual Reading Checkout.

> **Note:** All remedies are based on "averages" of the group. If individual students in your group fail to meet mastery criteria but the group consistently meets the criteria, you should provide additional catch-up practice for the students who are failing. An effective procedure is to arrange for other students to provide those students with an additional daily reading checkout.

In-Program Mastery Test Schedule

Test	Lesson Number	Possible Lesson Reviews
1	4	3, 4
2	7	6, 7
3	14	13, 14
4	17	16, 17
5	25	24, 25
6	35	Story-reading exercises for Lessons 31–34 and all of Lesson 35
7	40	Story-reading exercises for Lessons 36–39 and all of Lesson 40
8	45	Story-reading exercises for Lessons 41–44 and all of Lesson 45
9	50	Story-reading exercises for Lessons 46–49 and all of Lesson 50
10	55	Story-reading exercises for Lessons 51–54 and all of Lesson 55
11	60	Story-reading exercises for Lessons 56–59 and all of Lesson 60
12	65	Story-reading exercises for Lessons 61–64 and all of Lesson 65

Decoding Placement Test

Preparation

Reproduce one copy of the test for each student and each tester. A reproducible copy appears on pages 55 and 56 of this guide.

Administration

Select a quiet place to administer the test. Students who are to be tested later should not observe or hear another student being tested. You will need a test form for each student and a stopwatch or a watch with a second hand. When administering the test, sit across from the student. Position the test form so that the student cannot see what you are writing on the form.

Fill out the top lines of the test form (student information). Keep this filled-out test form and hand the student a clean copy of the test.

PART I

Tell the student Read this story out loud. Follow along with your finger so you don't lose your place. Read carefully. Begin timing as soon as the student begins reading the first sentence.

Record each decoding mistake the student makes in oral reading. Mark an X on the filled-out form to show where the student made each mistake.

◆ If the student omits a word, mark an X above the omitted word.

◆ If the student adds a word that does not appear in the story, mark an X between two words to show where the word had been added.

◆ If the student misidentifies a word, mark an X above the misidentified word. Do not count the same misidentified word more than once. (For example, if the student misidentified the name "Hurn" four times, count only 1 error.)

◆ If the student cannot identify a word within 3 seconds, say the word and mark an X above it.

◆ If the student makes a mistake and then self-corrects by saying the correct word, mark an X above the word.

◆ If the student sounds out a word but does not pronounce it at a normal speaking rate, ask What word? If the student does not identify it, mark an X above the word.

◆ Do not count the re-reading of a word or phrase as an error if the word is read correctly both times.

Note: If you wish to use diagnostic procedures, you can use additional code information to indicate the type of mistake the student makes. You may, for example, write **SC** above self-corrections, **SO** above sound-out mistakes, and **O** above omitted words. You may also wish to write in what the student calls the misidentified words or what the student adds.

After each of the word-identification errors, tell the student the correct word.

When recording the errors, make sure that your copy of the story is not visible to the student. The student should not be able to see the marks that you're making.

Stop timing as soon as the student completes the story.

Enter the total errors for Part I on the appropriate line at the top of the filled-in test form. Also record the time required by the student to read Part I.

Refer to the placement schedule for Part I to determine placement or whether you should administer another part of the test.

PART II

Part II is a series of sentences that are to be read aloud by the student. You do not need to time this part of the test. To administer, present the section labeled Part II and tell the student Read these sentences out loud. Follow along with your finger so you don't lose your place. Read carefully.

Record each decoding error the student makes while reading. When the student finishes reading Part II, enter the total errors for Part II on the appropriate line at the top

of the test form. Then determine the student's placement by referring to the placement schedule for Part II. Fill in the "Placement" blank at the top of the test form.

PARTS III and IV

Each of these test sections is a passage that is to be read aloud by the student and timed. To administer, present the appropriate section and tell the student I'm going to time your reading of this selection. Read out loud and read carefully. Record errors as specified for Part I.

When the student finishes reading Part III, enter the total errors and time required at the top of the test form. Then refer to the placement schedule for Part III to determine placement or whether you should administer Part IV.

When the student finishes reading Part IV, enter the total errors and time required at the top of the test form. Then determine the student's placement and fill in the "Placement" blank.

DECODING PLACEMENT SCHEDULE

ERRORS	TIME	PLACEMENT OR NEXT TEST
PART I		
22 or more	—	Administer PART II Test
12 to 21	more than 2:00	Level A, Lesson 1
12 to 21	2:00 or less	Administer PART II Test
0 to 11	more than 2:00	Level B1, Lesson 1
0 to 11	2:00 or less	Administer PART III Test
PART II		
41 or more	—	No **Corrective Reading** Placement; use a beginning reading program
8 to 40	—	Level A, Lesson 1
0 to 7	—	Level B1, Lesson 1
PART III		
15 or more	—	Level B1, Lesson 1
6 to 15	more than 2:30	Level B1, Lesson 1
6 to 15	2:30 or less	Level B2, Lesson 1
0 to 5	more than 2:30	Level B1, Lesson 1
0 to 5	2:30 or less	Administer PART IV Test
PART IV		
9 or more	—	Level B2, Lesson 1
4 to 8	more than 1:30	Level B2, Lesson 1
4 to 8	1:30 or less	Level C, Lesson 1
0 to 3	more than 1:20	Level C, Lesson 1
0 to 3	1:20 or less	Doesn't need **Corrective Reading** decoding program

SRA's Corrective Reading
Decoding Placement Test

Name _____ Class _____ Date _____

School _____ Tester _____

PART I   Errors _____   Time _____

PART II   Errors _____

PART III   Errors _____   Time _____

PART IV   Errors _____   Time _____

Placement: _____

PART I

Kit made a boat. She made the boat of tin. The nose of the boat was very thin. Kit said, "I think that this boat is ready for me to take on the lake." So Kit went to the lake with her boat.

Her boat was a lot of fun. It went fast. But when she went to dock it at the boat ramp, she did not slow it down. And the thin nose of the boat cut a hole in the boat ramp.

The man who sold gas at the boat ramp got mad. He said, "That boat cuts like a blade. Do not take the boat on this lake any more."

PART II

Can she see if it is dim?

And it can fit in a hand.

Now the hat is on her pet pig.

I sent her a clock last week.

How will we get dinner on this ship?

The swimming class went well.

When they met, he felt happy.

Then she told me how happy she was.

The tracks led to a shack next to the hill.

They said, "We will plant the last of the seeds."

What will you get when you go to the store?

You left lots of things on her desk.

PART III

Hurn was sleeping when it happened. Hurn didn't hear the big cat sneak into the cave that Hurn called his home. Suddenly Hurn was awake. Something told him, "Beware!" His eyes turned to the darkness near the mouth of the cave. Hurn felt the fur on the back of his neck stand up. His nose, like noses of all wolves, was very keen. It made him very happy when it smelled something good. But now it smelled something that made him afraid.

Hurn was five months old. He had never seen a big cat. He had seen clover and ferns and grass. He had even eaten rabbits. Hurn's mother had come back with them after she had been out hunting. She had always come back. And Hurn had always been glad to see her. But now she was not in the cave. Hurn's sister, Surt, was the only happy smell that reached Hurn's nose.

PART IV

During a good year, a large redwood will produce over six kilograms of seed, which is nearly a million and a half seeds. And the year that our redwood seed fluttered from the cone was an exceptionally good year. The parent tree produced over eight kilograms of seed that year, enough seed to start a forest that would be ten square kilometers in size. However, only a few redwood seeds survived. In fact, only three of the seeds from the parent tree survived their first year, and only one of them lived beyond the first year.

Obviously, our seed was lucky. It was a fortunate seed because it was fertile. If a seed is not fertile, it cannot grow, and about nine out of every ten redwood seeds are not fertile. Our seed also had the advantage of landing in a place where it could survive. If it had fallen on a part of the forest floor covered with thick, heavy litter, it probably would not have grown. If it had fluttered to a spot that became too dry during the summer, it would have died during the first year. Our seed landed in a spot where moles had been digging.

Scope and Sequence Chart

The Scope and Sequence Chart provides an overview of the skills taught in **Decoding A.** The skills are divided into three principal areas: word-attack skills, Workbook exercises, and support activities. The chart indicates which lessons offer practice in a given skill. The chart also shows where Mastery Tests and Individual Reading Checkouts are presented.

WORD-ATTACK SKILLS

Sound Identification	1
Pronunciations	1
Say the Sounds	1
Word Reading	1

WORKBOOK EXERCISES

Sound Dictation	1
Sound It Out	1 4
Word Reading: Workbook	5
Word Completion	6
Word Copying	6
Spelling from Dictation	
Sentence Reading	
Story Reading	

SUPPORT ACTIVITIES

Matching Sounds	1 8
Matching and Copying Sounds	1
Matching Completion	9
Circle Game	1

**CHECKOUTS
MASTERY TESTS**

Individual Reading Checkouts	1
In-Program Mastery Tests	4 7
Supplemental Mastery Tests	

LESSONS 1–65

65

65

10

65

65

42 44 47 50 52 54 60 62 65

65

25

26 65

18 65

30 65

11

65

42 44 47 50 52 54 60 62 65

46 (Timed Reading Checkouts) 65

14 17 25 35 40 45 50 55 60 65

20 45 65

Behavioral Objectives

The following chart gives specific information for each skill taught in **Decoding A.** Three columns of information are provided. The **BEHAVIORAL OBJECTIVE** column details the kind of performance that can be expected from a student who has mastered the skill. The column headed **The student is asked to** describes the tasks the student performs in order to master the skill. The **LESSONS** column shows the lessons in which the skill appears.

Word-Attack Skills

Sound Identification

BEHAVIORAL OBJECTIVE	The student is asked to	LESSONS
The student learns the sound made by each letter of the alphabet.	1) View a letter as the teacher says its sound; 2) say the letter's sound.	1–65 (See table on page 20 for a list of sounds and sound combinations.)
The student is able to read a letter and say its sound.	Orally read letters that the teacher points to.	1–65
The student learns sounds made by certain letter combinations.	1) View a letter combination as the teacher says its sound; 2) say the letter combination's sound.	1–65 (See table on page 20 for a list of sounds and sound combinations.)
The student is able to read a letter combination and say its sound.	Orally read a letter combination that the teacher points to.	9–65

• Appendix C •

Pronunciations

BEHAVIORAL OBJECTIVE	The student is asked to	LESSONS
The student is able to pronounce individual sounds.	Repeat individual sounds spoken by the teacher.	1–5
The student is able to pronounce individual words.	Repeat individual words spoken by the teacher.	1–27, 29, 32–42, 44–47, 50–65
When presented with a group of words with a common vowel sound, the student is able to pronounce the sound.	1) Repeat a group of words spoken by the teacher; 2) pronounce their common vowel sound.	1–13, 18–27
When presented with a group of words with different vowel sounds, the student is able to identify which word has a particular sound.	1) Repeat a group of words spoken by the teacher; 2) listen to a vowel sound spoken by the teacher; 3) say the word that has the same vowel sound.	4–65
When presented with a group of similar-sounding words, the student is able to identify the meaning of each word.	1) Repeat a group of similar-sounding words spoken by the teacher; 2) listen to a definition of one of the words; 3) identify the defined word.	50–52, 54–60, 62–65

Say the Sounds

The student is able to sound out a word and then say it at a normal rate.	1) Repeat a word spoken slowly by the teacher; 2) say the word at a normal rate.	1–10

Word Reading

The student is able to sound out a written word and then read the word at a normal rate.	1) Sound out a written word; 2) orally read the word at a normal rate.	1–24

Word Reading cont.

BEHAVIORAL OBJECTIVE	The student is asked to	LESSONS
The student is able to read a word at a normal rate.	Orally read a word at a normal rate, without sounding it out.	16–65
The student is able to determine whether a word has a short or a long *e* sound.	1) View a word with a short or a long *e* sound; 2) say the sound; 3) orally read the word.	23–32
The student is able to determine whether a word has a short or long *o* sound.	1) View a word with a short or a long *o* sound; 2) say the sound; 3) orally read the word.	32–36
The student learns how to read certain irregularly spelled words.	1) View the word as the teacher reads it; 2) sound out the word; 3) orally read the word.	36*(I);* 47–49 *(was, to);* 52–54 *(do, said);* 56–58 *(of, you, what)*

Workbook Exercises

Sound Dictation

BEHAVIORAL OBJECTIVE	The student is asked to	LESSONS
Upon hearing a sound, the student is able to write the letter or letter combination that makes the sound.	1) Listen to a sound; 2) write the letter or letter combination that makes the sound.	1–65

Sound It Out

The student is able to sound out a written word.	Sound out a written word.	1–4

Word Reading: Workbook

BEHAVIORAL OBJECTIVE	The student is asked to	LESSONS
The student is able to sound out a written word and then read the word at a normal rate.	1) Sound out a written word; 2) orally read the word at a normal rate.	5–16
The student is able to read a word at a normal rate.	Orally read a word at a normal rate, without sounding it out.	17–21
The student is able to identify underlined sounds in words.	1) Identify an underlined sound in a word; 2) orally read the word at a normal rate.	22–42, 44–47, 50–52, 54–60, 62–65

Word Completion

The student is able to write a dictated word by adding letters to a short or incomplete word.	1) View a short or incomplete word; 2) listen to a word dictated by the teacher; 3) write the dictated word by adding letters to the short or incomplete word.	6–65
The student is able to write a dictated word by first writing part of the word and then the entire word.	1) Write a short or incomplete word dictated by the teacher; 2) write a dictated word by adding letters to the short or incomplete word.	21–31

Word Copying

The student is able to copy a written word.	1) View a list of words; 2) identify and copy a word spoken by the teacher.	6–25

• Appendix C •

Spelling from Dictation

BEHAVIORAL OBJECTIVE	The student is asked to	LESSONS
The student is able to write a dictated word.	Write a word dictated by the teacher.	22–65

Sentence Reading

The student is able to read a sentence.	1) Orally read a sentence, pausing before each word; 2) orally read the sentence without pauses.	18–22
The student is able to read a group of sentences	1) Orally read a group of sentences, pausing before each word; 2) orally read one sentence without pauses.	23–65
The student is able to answer comprehension questions about a sentence.	1) Follow along as the teacher reads a sentence; 2) answer comprehension questions about the sentence.	18–29
The student learns the function of quotation marks within a sentence.	1) Orally read a sentence with quotation marks; 2) orally read the quote.	53, 54
The student is able to read a story.	1) Orally read a story, pausing before each word; 2) orally read the story without pauses.	30–65
The student is able to answer comprehension questions about a story.	1) Follow along as the teacher reads the story; 2) answer comprehension questions about the story.	30–65
The student is able to answer comprehension questions about story illustrations.	Answer comprehension questions about story illustrations.	30–39, 41, 42

Support Activities

Matching Sounds

BEHAVIORAL OBJECTIVE	The student is asked to	LESSONS
When presented with two columns of letters, the student is able to identify the matching letters.	Draw a line from a letter in the first column to its matching letter in the second column.	1–8

Matching and Copying Sounds

The student is able to copy letters.	1) View a letter; 2) follow a line connected to the letter; 3) copy the letter in a blank at the end of the line.	1–11

Matching Completion

The student is able to make two written words match by adding a letter to one of the words.	1) View a pair of words; 2) make the words match by adding a letter to one of the words.	9–11
The student is able to copy a column of written words.	1) View a column of words; 2) copy the entire column.	12–46
The student is able to make two words match by adding two or more letters to one of the words.	1) View a pair of words; 2) make the words match by adding two or more letters to one of the words.	47–65

Circle Game

When presented with a row of letters, the student is able to identify the letters that make a given sound.	1) Read a circled letter or letter combination; 2) view a row of letters; 3) circle the letters in the row that are the same as the circled letter(s).	1–32
When presented with a row of letters, the student is able to identify the consecutive letters in a row that spell a given word.	1) Read a circled word; 2) view a row of letters; 3) circle the consecutive letters in the row that spell the word.	33–42, 44–47, 50–52, 54–60, 62–65

Checkouts and Mastery Tests

Individual Reading Checkouts

BEHAVIORAL OBJECTIVE	The student is asked to	LESSONS
The student is able to sound out words.	Sound out a list of words while making no more than 1 error.	1–4
The student is able to sound out words and then read them at a normal rate.	Sound out a list of words and then read them at a normal rate, while making no more than 1 error.	5–22
The student is able to read sentences orally.	Orally read a group of sentences while making no more than 1 error.	23–29
The student is able to read a story orally.	Orally read a story while making no more than 1 error.	30–45
The student is able to read a story orally within a specific time limit.	Orally read a story in one minute or less, while making no more than 2 errors.	46–65

In-Program Mastery Tests

The student is able to demonstrate mastery of skills presented in the program.	Take mastery tests that measure the student's mastery of skills presented in the program.	4, 7, 14, 17, 25, 35, 40, 45, 50, 55, 60, 65

Skills Profile Chart

The Skills Profile Chart can be used to record an individual student's mastery of each skill taught in **Decoding A.** The chart summarizes the skills presented in the program and provides space for indicating when a student has mastered each skill. One copy of the chart should be made for each student in the class.

Name _____

Word-Attack Skills

SKILLS	LESSON RANGE	DATE MASTERED
Sound Identification Learns sound(s) made by each letter of the alphabet	1–59	
Reads a letter and says its sound	1–65	
Learns sounds made by letter combinations *(th, sh, ing, ck, wh, ol, er, or, ch, qu)*	9–62	
Reads a letter combination and says its sound	9–65	
Pronunciations Repeats individual sounds	1–5	
Repeats individual words	1–65	
Repeats a group of words and pronounces their common vowel sound	1–27	
Repeats a group of words and identifies which word has a given sound	4–65	
Repeats a group of similar-sounding words and identifies each word's meaning	50–65	
Say the Sounds Repeats a sounded-out word; says the word at a normal rate	1–10	
Word Reading Sounds out a written word; orally reads the word at a normal rate	1–24	
Orally reads a word at a normal rate, without sounding it out	16–65	
Determines whether a word has a short or a long *e* sound	23–32	
Determines whether a word has a short or a long *o* sound	32–36	
Learns how to read certain irregular words *(I, was, to, do, said, of, you, what)*	36–58	

Workbook Exercises

SKILLS	LESSON RANGE	DATE MASTERED
Sound Dictation Writes the letter or letter combination that makes a dictated sound	1–65	
Sound It Out Sounds out a written word	1–4	
Word Reading: Workbook Sounds out a written word; orally reads the word at a normal rate	5–16	
Orally reads a word at a normal rate, without sounding it out	17–21	
Identifies an underlined sound in a word; orally reads the word at a normal rate	22–65	

Workbook Exercises *cont.*

SKILLS	LESSON RANGE	DATE MASTERED
Word Completion Writes a dictated word by adding letters to a short or incomplete word	6-65	
Writes a dictated word by first writing part of the word and then the entire word	21-31	
Word Copying Identifies and copies written words	6-25	
Spelling from Dictation Writes a dictated word	26-65	
Sentence Reading Orally reads a sentence	18-22	
Orally reads a group of sentences	23-65	
Answers comprehension questions about a sentence	18-29	
Learns the function of quotation marks within a sentence	53-54	
Story Reading Orally reads a story	30-65	
Answers comprehension questions about a story	30-65	
Answers comprehension questions about story illustrations	30-42	

Support Activities

SKILLS	LESSON RANGE	DATE MASTERED
Matching Sounds Draws lines between matching letters	1-8	
Matching and Copying Sounds Copies letters	1-11	
Matching Completion Makes two written words match by adding a letter to one of the words	9-11	
Copies a column of written words	12-46	
Makes two written words match by adding two or more letters to one of the words	47-65	
Circle Game Circles letters that make a given sound	1-32	
Circles letters that spell a given word	33-65	

Checkouts/Mastery Tests

SKILLS	LESSON RANGE	DATE MASTERED
Individual Reading Checkouts Sounds out a list of words within an error limit	1-4	
Orally reads a list of words within an error limit	5-22	
Orally reads a group of sentences within an error limit	23-29	
Orally reads a story within an error limit	30-45	
Orally reads a story within a time and error limit	46-65	
Mastery Tests Demonstrates mastery of skills presented in the program	4-65	